Ján Lacika

PRAGUE

A tourist guide

PRÍRODA

Dr. Ján Lacika (1956) was born in Prague. He has been actively working in the field of geography and environmental sciences. Besides his scientific work, he is dedicated to photography, drawing maps, and writing popular scientific and tourist books. He lives in Bratislava, although he has traveled to most European countries. He attended the British Royal Holloway University of London for an academic year.

Contents

Beneath the Old Town Hall Clock

INTRODUCTION

According to an old Czech legend, the Bohemian Princess Libuše once made a great prophecy: 'I see a great city, whose glory will touch the stars.' At least 12 centuries later, we can say that her prophecy has been fulfilled to the letter. Prague really is famous throughout the whole world. One of Europe's most beautiful cities, it has been given many names, such as the 'mother of all cities', 'golden Prague' and 'Prague of a hundred spires'. Each of these names has a large helping of truth contained within them, reflecting the city's charm and uniqueness. People come from all over the world to see for themselves whether the claims about the beauty of the Czech capital are true. Prague has much to offer tourists, and this is reflected by the fact that in 1992 the historical centre of the city was included on the exclusive UNESCO cultural heritage list.

Hradčany and the Lesser Town from the Bridge Tower

Prague is the capital of the Czech Republic, the home of the president, government and parliament. Within its 496 square kilometres live 1.177 million inhabitants (June 30, 2005). The territory of Greater Prague forms one self-contained administrative unit. It is divided into 22 administrative districts and 57 parts.

Prague of a Hundred Spires

Prague is renowned for its towers. It is no accident that it is called Prague of a hundred spires. It even has towers on its coat of arms. The 'hundred spires' name was given to the city in the 19th century by the Italian Bernardo Bolzani, who took the trouble to count the towers and came up with the figure 103. Today there are many more, it is thought that there are around 500. Around a dozen of the towers can be climbed in order to get a good overview of the city. You can chose between the main tower of St. Vitus Cathedral (pg 17), Petrin Watchtower (pg 24), the bell-tower of the Church of St. Nicholas (pg 26), both towers on Charles Bridge, Old Town Hall (pg 33), Powder Gate (pg 35), Klementinum Astronomical Tower (pg 37), New Town Hall (pg 48), Žižkov Television Tower (pg 60).

The Vltava river from Letná

ENVIRONMENT

Geography

Prague's location can be summed up in one word – central. It lies in the centre of both Europe and the country of which it is the capital city. The nearest border town of Cínovec is 101 km away, while the most distant – Jablunkov is almost 400km from the city. As the Czech Republic is not a large country, Prague isn't too far away from other large European cities such as Dresden – 160 km, Vienna – 300 km, Bratislava – 320 km, Berlin – 350 km, Munich – 360 km, Krakow – 500 km, Budapest – 550 km, Warsaw – 630 km, and Zurich – 670 km. The city lies exactly 50 degrees north – the same as Krakow in Poland, Lvov in Ukraine, and Winnipeg in Canada – and 14' 25' 17' east.

Climate

Prague's climate is determined by its position in the middle of Europe, although the prevailing wind comes from the Atlantic Ocean. Weather fronts from the west bring cool and damp air. For this reason the weather in Prague is best described as changeable. At any time of the year you can be lucky and find warm, sunny weather, but several days of rain and grey skies can't be ruled out either. Although the weather is changeable, there are certain long-recorded peculiarities. For example, *Medard's raindrops* (the rainy beginning of summer) or *grandma's summer* (a dry and sunny autumn). The nicest time of year in Prague is the summer, thanks to the high temperatures and the long daylight hours, but even the snowy winter has its own special charm. The rich cultural treasures on offer, however, mean that you are not forced to plan your visit to Prague according to the time of year or the weather. Even the most overcast and rainy days can be spent pleasantly in the city's museums, art galleries, cinemas, theatres or over a beer in a quaint Prague pub.

Relief

Prague certainly can't be called a hilly city, with no mountains for many miles. On the other hand, it is by no means as flat as Moscow or Amsterdam. There aren't any hills as such, even though the view from the Vltava river may give this impression. The high ground is actually only the edge of a wide undulating plain, which covers most of the city suburbs. The highest point is the Teleček rise (399m) near Sobín on the western edge of the city. The lowest point, at 177m above sea level is on the banks of the Vltava river at Suchdol in the north of Prague. The city is not

Bridges on the Vltava river

completely flat thanks to the Vltava river, which cut a moderately deep valley into the plain. In places it flows past steep rocky slopes (for example, the Barandov Rocks). The river enters the city to the south through a narrow valley, which at Vyšehrad broadens out on the right bank into a small basin on which the Old and New Towns are found.

After a large bend, which curves around Holešovice, the valley closes in again, before the Vltava flows out of the city to the north. The Vltava's tributaries have also formed romantic natural features, such as the deep gully cut by the Šárecký stream in the northwest of the city, which the locals often visit on Sundays.

The Royal Gardens with Summerhouse

Statue representing the Vltava river

The Vltava River

Prague and the Vltava river are inseparable. It would be difficult to imagine the Czech capital without the country's longest river, which flows down from the Šumava Mountains. The Vltava flows through Prague for 31 km, dividing the city into two parts, with around one third of the land on the left (west) bank, and the other two thirds on the right (east). The river gracefully flows from south to north, maintaining this direction apart from a large bend that begins beneath the Charles Bridge. At Trója, the Vltava returns to its original course. The river basin reaches a width of 300 metres.

Prague Parks and Gardens

Fortunately, in this densely built city there is also room for greenery. Prague's parks and gardens cover an area of 870 hectares. In the big city you can find attractive 'islands of green' set aside for relaxation and sport. The most popular are the English-style Stromovka Park in Holešovice, the Summer Gardens ('Letenské sady') in the neighbouring Hradčany, Petřín Park and the Star Hunting Ground with its

The Kinský Garden

summer house of the same name just past Břevnov. The most beautiful gardens are probably those in the Lesser Town. The green lungs of the city are found in Kundratice woods to the southeast and the woods in the Šárka valley in the west. The most valued of these locations are set aside as natural reserves and other protected zones.

HISTORY

Prehistoric Prague

When searching for the origins of Prague before the 9th century AD, we have to rely on the authenticity of various legends and the work of archaeologists. The rich archaeological finds suggest that the territory of today's Prague has attracted interest from

The Celtic Závist Fort

The Celts in the Prague area had their main base in the southern part of the modern city territory. In the Závist district on the Vltava river's right-bank (opposite Zbraslava) archaeologists discovered what was probably the largest Celtic fort in Bohemia. The Boii stronghold covered an area of 170 hectares. The fort contained a mint in which gold and silver Celtic coins were produced, and nowadays you can take a tour of the fort.

The Kosmas Chronicle

The writings of Czech chronicler Kosmas form the oldest written record of the Czech nation. Their author is the also the first Czech writer who we know by name. Kosmas (probably 1045-1125) was not only a chronicler, but also the Dean of the St. Vitus Cathedral Chapter House, and often served as the king's personal envoy. The Kosmas Chronicle, written in Latin and in three volumes, provides a history of the Czechs from their coming to power until Kosmas's own time, i.e. the beginning of the 12th century. Many of the historical events and perhaps even figures in the Kosmas Chronicle represent fodder for doubt, as indeed, they are drawn from stories and legends, touching on a period stretching back three centuries. Despite this, the chronicle should be considered as significant, if only from the literary point of view. It was something like a historical novel, a precursor to similar works written by the greatest Czech historical novelist Alois Jirásek eight centuries later.

St. Wenceslas

Methodius. The prince moved his capital to the Levý Hradec fort, which then stood on the site of today's Prague Castle. The rulers then began to develop the area around the fort, which was faithfully recorded by a merchant called Ibrahim Ibn Jakub in 965. This Jewish traveller from Moorish Spain spoke of the 'rich city of *Fraga*', with its whitewashed houses made of stone and busy marketplaces.

Romanesque Prague

The Bohemian Premyslid dynasty ruled from Prague until the beginning of the 14th century. During this period the Bohemian kingdom became an important and influential state in Central Europe. This was reflected by the rapid growth of Prague. During the reign of the Přemysl Otakar II it was the capital of a state stretching beyond the borders of the modern-day Czech Republic. For a considerable time, Prague

prehistoric times. For thousands of years cultures replaced each other, until in the 6th century B.C. we find the first group that can be properly identified. At this time, Prague became a part of the Celtic world, on land belonging to a Boii tribe, after whom the Romans named the territory of the current Czech Republic *Bohemia*. Even today this name is widely known. After the Celts, came the Germanic Markomani and Longobardi tribes, who provided a constant threat to the Roman Empire.

Old Slavic Prague

At some time in the 6th century A.D. the first Slavic tribes arrived in the Bohemian basin. The dominant group in the area became the Czechs. The oldest history of the Slavs in Prague until around the 9th century is surrounded by old stories and legends. Their authenticity cannot be checked against written sources, which are missing. According to the Kosmas Chronicle from the 11th century (see below), Prague was founded by Princess Libuše, whose marriage to a peasant called Přemysl the Ploughman led to the founding of the ruling Premyslid dynasty. Legend has it that the princess sent a messenger into the woods near the Vltava river in order to find someone who was in the process of building a house. They found a man who was shaping the threshold of his home, which is why the city was named Prague. (In the Czech language the word for threshold is 'prah', while Prague is called 'Praha'). The first figures in Czech history that can definitely be identified are Prince Bořivoj I and his wife St. Ludmila. Both were baptised around 884 in Moravia by St.

Chronology

5th – 1st century B.C. – Territory of Prague settled by Celtic Boii tribe, whose main base was Závist fort.
1st – 5th centuries A.D. – Prague settled by Germanic tribes Markomani and Longobardi
6th century A.D. – The first Slavs arrive in Prague.
After 870 A.D. – Prince Bořivoj I founds Prague Castle.
965 A.D. – Merchant Ibn Jakub writes about the city of *Fraga*.
973 A.D. – Prince Boleslav II founds the Prague bishopric at St. Vitus Cathedral in Prague Castle.

developed as a free association of five autonomous towns. In the middle of the 13th century, it had around 4,000 inhabitants. The centre of Romanesque Prague became the Old Town on the right bank of the Vltava river. In the 13th century the so-called Havel Town grew on the southern side. Next to this part of the city two independent Jewish towns were created. In the south was the fortified Vyše-hrad, which from 1061-1092 was the ruler's main residence. On the left bank the towns of Hradčany and the Lesser Town grew up on a small piece of land by Prague Castle, which became the main residence of the king and the bishop of Prague. The Vltava river was spanned in 1170 by Judith Bridge, which was made of stone. The city also contained two important monasteries – the Břevnov Monastery founded in 993 and the Strahov Monastery founded in 1140.

The Left Embankment

St. George Basilica

Romanesque Buildings

St. George Basilica (Prague Castle) (pg 17)
Remains of a Romanesque palace beneath
the Royal Palace (Prague Castle) (pg 18)
St. Cross Rotunda (Old Town) (pg 38)
Remains of a courtyard beneath the house
of the gentleman from Kunštát (Old Town)
(pg 38)
St. Longin Rotunda (New Town) (pg 49)
St. Martin Rotunda (Vyšehrad) (pg 52)

Gothic Prague

Prague's golden age can be said to have begun in
the 14th century, with the city enjoying the benevo-
lent rule of Charles IV. This wise ruler raised his
beloved city to among the largest and most developed European centres. It is thought that around

Charles IV

*King Charles IV (1326-1378) is recognised as
one of the most important figures in Czech
history to this day, even winning a television
vote to find the 'Greatest Czech'. Although
his father was from the house of Luxembourg, thanks to his mother Eliška Přemyslovna he had a close relationship with
the Czechs. When he became the Holy Roman Emperor, he chose Prague as his capital,
and turned it into the most beautiful city in
Europe. The reign of Charles IV was a golden
age in the history of both Prague and the
whole of Bohemia. His grateful subjects
dubbed him 'the Father of the Nation'.*

Charles IV

Chronology

1085 – Vratislav I becomes the first Czech
king, ruling from Prague Castle.
After 1230 – The Old Town emerges as
the first Prague town.
1257 – The Lesser Town becomes
Prague's second town.
1306 – The murder of Wenceslas III in
Olomouc puts an end to the Premyslid
dynasty rule in Bohemia. John of
Luxembourg takes the vacant throne.
1320 – Hradčany becomes the third town
in Prague.

80,000 people lived in the city at this time. Thanks to Charles IV, the city grew with the addition of the New Town and the Charles Bridge, and Prague became an archbishopric – the first in Central Europe. The splendid St. Vitus Cathedral enriched the king's residence at Prague Castle. Prague was less fortunate in the 15th century, with the Hussite uprising. From the Bethlehem Chapel the Hussites sent forth their call for the reform of the Catholic Church, and on the Vítkov Hill at the gates of the city they won their first battle with the forces of the Church. Hussite Prague then had to bear the negative results of the revolt. Its economic and urban development was halted, poverty spread among the people, churches and monasteries were burnt down.

Chronology

1346-1378 – Reign of Charles IV, Prague flourishes.
1344 – Prague bishopric becomes archbishopric.
1348 – Charles IV founds Prague University and New Town.
1402-1413 – Jan Hus preaches in Bethlehem Chapel.
June 30, 1419 – 'Defenestration' (throwing something or someone from a window) of councillors at the New Town Town Hall marks the beginning of the Hussite uprising.
July 14, 1420 – Hussites defeat the Catholic Crusaders at the Battle of Vítkov.
1420-1434 – Hussite Wars reach Prague.
March 2, 1458 – Hussite King George of Poděbrady ascends to Bohemian throne. First coronation procession follows the King's Way.

Gothic Buildings

St. Vitus Cathedral (Prague Castle) (pg 16)
Vladislav Hall in the Royal Palace (Prague Castle) (pg 18)
Charles Bridge and Tower (linking the Lesser Town and the Old Town) (pg 29)
Old Town Hall Tower (Old Town) (pg 32)
Tyn Church (Old Town) (pg 33)
The Stone Bell House (Old Town) (pg 33)
Powder Gate (Old Town) (pg 35)
Old-New Synagogue (Josefov) (pg 39)
Church of the Virgin Mary of the Snow (New Town) (pg 41)

16th and 17th Century Prague

After the Reformation, Prague experienced the Renaissance, which accompanied the first Hapsburg ruler of the Czech lands – Ferdinand I. It was in his reign that Prague began to be built in the Italian

St. Vitus Cathedral

Charles IV in St. Vitus Cathedral

Jan Hus defends his teachings

style, especially within the Royal Gardens. The height of the Renaissance in the city was the reign of Rudolf II (1584-1611) – a reign that ushered in a second golden age.

Renaissance Monuments

Rudolf II.

The Spanish Hall (Prague Castle) (pg 15)
Golden Lane (Prague Castle) (pg 18)
The Royal Summerhouse (Hradčany) (pg 19)
The Smiřický Palace (Lesser Town) (pg 26)
Schwarzenberg Palace (Hradčany) (pg 26)
The Granovský House in Ungelt (Old Town) (pg 33)
The Star Summerhouse (White Hill) (pg 56)

The Baroque Style came to Prague in the hard times of the 17th century. In 1619, the Czech noblemen rose up against the Hapsburgs, but suffered a crushing defeat at the fateful Battle of the White Hill to the west of Prague. The Thirty Years War kept Prague at a practical standstill for many years. It was only in the second half of the 17th century that the political situation stabilised and Prague's economy and society came back to life. Baroque became an effective weapon of the Catholic Hapsburgs in their struggle with the Protestants, which is why it was allowed free reign. The Church built Baroque churches, while the noblemen loyal to the emperors built luxurious palaces. The Baroque style radically changed the medieval appearance of many old churches.

Baroque portal on Nerudova Street

Rudolf II

The Emperor Rudolf II (1552-1612) was the third Hapsburg ruler of Bohemia. The king suffered from a persecution complex, which is why he never married. Rudolf had little interest in politics, devoting himself to pleasure, mainly the arts and alchemy. He was given the nickname 'the alchemist monarch'. He chose Prague Castle as his residence, and it was here that he placed his renowned art collection. The emperor's court included artists, scientists and charlatans. The court alchemists attempted to turn stones into gold, and discover the elixir of youth. Among the frauds, however, were some genuine greats, including Tycho de Brahe and Johannes Kepler. Rudolf was never destined to die as an emperor and king. A few months before he died he was forced to abdicate by his brother Mathias.

Baroque Monuments

The Loreta (Hradčany) (pg 22)
Church of St. Nicholas (Lesser Town) (pg 26)
The Valdštejn Palace and Gardens (Lesser Town) (pg 27)
The Charles Bridge Statues (pg 29)
The Old-Town Church of St. Nicholas (Old Town) (pg 33)
The Vyšehrad Citadel (Vyšehrad) (pg 52)
Troja Castle (Troja) (pg 58)

Chronology

1526 – Reign of the Hapsburgs in the Czech lands begins, lasting until 1918.
1584-1611 – Reign of Hapsburg Emperor Rudolf II from Prague Castle.
1598-1609 – Chief Rabbi of Prague is the Renowned Rabbi Low, credited with creating the Golem.
May 23, 1618 – Group of Protestants 'defenestrate' Catholic governors from the windows of the Royal Palace in Prague Castle. Thirty Years War begins.
November 8, 1620 – Hapsburg troops defeat rebel Czech noblemen at the Battle of the White Hill.
June 21, 1621 – Execution of 27 leaders of rebel Czech Protestants on Old Town Square.
July 25, 1648 – Swede troops capture Prague Castle. End of Thirty Years War.
1653 – Jesuits come to Prague and build the Clementinum.

Chronology

May 12, 1743 – Maria Theresia crowned as Czech Queen in Prague.
1760 – Prague Castle Moat filled in.
1784 – Merging of four towns of form unified Prague.
October 29, 1787 – Mozart himself attends the premiere of his opera 'Don Giovanni' at the Estates Theatre.
1848 – People of Prague take part in the revolutionary uprisings sweeping Europe.
August 12, 1881 – Shortly after the building work is completed, a fire breaks out at the National Theatre building. The Grand Opening is delayed to September 18, 1883.
1891 – Jubilee Exhibition takes place in Prague. Petřín Watchtower and Industrial Palace opened on Exhibition Ground.

Jubilee Exhibition

The citizens of Prague have often viewed the city as their great template. This was no exception at the Jubilee Exhibition in 1891, which came in response to the great success of the World Exhibition in Paris in 1889. A special exhibition ground was constructed on the eastern edge of the former Royal Hunting Ground (today's Stromovka) in Holešovice. The exhibition, visited by two and a half million people including Emperor Franz Joseph II, was a splendid showcase for the latest scientific and technical achievements of the age. It was thanks to this exhibition that Prague acquired the Industrial Palace built on the exhibition ground, the 'Prague Eiffel Tower' – the Petřín Watchtower, and the Hanavský Pavilion in the Letná Gardens.

18th and 19th Centuries

Baroque continued to be style of building in Prague in the 18th century, and for this reason it is this style that dominates the historical centre of the city. During the reign of Maria Theresia, however, the style mellowed somewhat into rococo. The Imperial and classicist forms were expressed in designs from antiquity and geometric lines. During the reign of Joseph II the people of Prague were allowed more religious freedoms, while the influence of the Catholic Church weakened. Prague became a centre of European culture and art. The merging of Prague's four towns in 1784 only confirmed that the city had long before grown into a single urban space. The main centre of life in the united Prague shifted from the Old Town to the New Town, which better suited the demands of a modern city.

In the 19th century Prague experienced the industrial revolution, which brought in great economic and social changes and radically altered the size and form of the city. Prague became the centre of the Czech national revival, which spread to the rest of the Czech lands. The Czech national consciousness was greatly boosted by the building of the National Theatre and the founding of various institutions mainly centred on Prague. The Czech phenomenon began to rival the German culture, which was preferred by official circles in Vienna. At the turn of the 20th century many buildings sprung up in the historicist and Art Nouveau style.

Inside the Ungelt

Monuments in the Historicist Style

Western Side and Tower of St. Vitus Cathedral (pg 16)
Rudolfinium (Old Town) (pg 41)
The National Museum (New Town) (pg 43)
The National Theatre (New Town) (pg 47)
Church of St. Peter and St. Paul (Vyšehrad) (pg 51)

Monuments in the Art Nouveau Style

Jan Hus Memorial (Old Town) (pg 32)
Municipal House (Old Town) (pg 35)
Hotel Evropa (New Town) (pg 44)

Modern Prague

Life in Prague in the 20th century was like a seesaw, with good times alternating with bad. The people of Prague experienced the end of the Hapsburg monarchy, two world wars, forty years of communist totalitarian rule and two periods of democracy and prosperity. In 1918, Prague became the capital of the newly formed Czechoslovakia. In a favourable social and economic climate during the interwar period it became a modern European metropolis. In 1920, the merging of 38 districts created Greater Prague with its almost 700,000 inhabitants. During WWII, Prague suffered under the cruel Nazi jackboot, but was lucky to escape the destruction that hit Warsaw and Dresden. There was fighting in the streets right up until the end of the war, with the May uprising of 1945. A coup in February 1948 ushered in more than 40 years of Communist rule. During this period, the city underwent massive development, and in 1961 the number of its inhabitants reached 1 million. A further expansion took place in 1974, when the city swallowed up another 30 surrounding districts. One positive development during the period was the building of the Prague Metro. Soviet tanks in August 1968 crushed the movement toward freedom and democracy, but in November 1989, Prague, along with the rest of Czechoslovakia finally managed to throw off the communist yoke. Today, Prague is the modern capital of a democratic Czech Republic, itself a member of the European Union.

Modern Architecture

House of the Black Madonna (Old Town) (pg 34)
The Dancing House (New Town) (pg 48)
Emmaus Church Tower (New Town) (pg 49)
Nusel Bridge (Nusle, Vyšehrad) (pg 49)
Congress Palace (Vyšehrad) (pg 50)
Trade Fair Palace (Holešovice) (pg 53)

Chronology

October 28, 1918 – Prague becomes the capital of Czechoslovakia following declaration in the Smetana Hall of the Municipal House.
March 15, 1939 – Army of Nazi Germany occupies Prague. Reich Protector rules Protectorate of Bohemia and Moravia from Prague Castle.
May 27, 1942 – Assassination of Reich Protector Reinhard Heydrich leads to great fascist terror against Czech citizens.
May 5-9, 1945 – Prague citizens rise up against Nazis and fight for four days before Soviet tanks liberate the city.
February 25, 1948 – Communists come to power in Prague, and rule over Czechs and Slovaks for 41 years.
August 21, 1968 – Warsaw Pact troops occupy Prague and the whole of Czechoslovakia, ending the hopeful period of democratisation known as the *Prague Spring*.
November 17, 1989 – Attack by Communist security units on students marks beginning of mass demonstrations, which led to the fall of the totalitarian regime in Czechoslovakia.
January 1, 1993 – Prague becomes the capital city of an independent Czech Republic.

Vítkov National Memorial (Žižkov) (pg 60)
Žižkov Television Tower (Žižkov) (pg 60)
Church of the Sacred Heart (Vinohrady) (pg 55)

Entrance to Budějovická metro station

On Wenceslas Square

PRAGUE CASTLE AND HRADČANY

For Czechs, Hradčany is the country's most sacred place, where Czech statehood emerged and where the country's most important historical events took place. It was the third Prague town to be founded, in 1320. Although it wasn't a free royal town, it still thrived. The attractive residences built for emperors, kings, princes and governors affected the surrounding area, as all the important people in the country wanted to live nearby. This means that Hradčany was full of the palaces of high noblemen and leading churchmen. Today, apart from being the site of the President's Palace, it is a place mainly where tourists gather.

Prague Castle

Prague Castle is without doubt among the most important monuments in Prague. It's the largest castle complex in the Czech Republic, and has been the political centre of the state for twelve centuries. It's where the Crown Jewels are kept, along with the mortal remains of many Czech rulers. Prague Castle is a unique collection of secular and religious buildings of extraordinary architectural and artistic value. Its history began around the ninth century. The first lord of the castle was Prince Bořivoj, who, some time after 870, declared it to be the main seat of the Premyslid royal house. Prague Castle was the birthplace of the city of the same name.

Most people enter the castle complex from Hradčany Square, on its west side. **Mathias Gate**(1),** with its richly decorated portals, connects the first two castle courtyards. This structure, built in 1614, was one of the first secular Baroque monuments in the Czech Republic. **The New Royal Palace**(2),** which runs along the other side of the courtyard, is rather austere looking. It was built at the time of the reconstruction work between 1753-1775. In the northern wing is the typical Spanish Hall, in which the Hapsburg Emperor Rudolf II (1552-1612) kept his favourite Spanish horses. Apart from his horses and alchemists, the eccentric ruler also had a weakness for art. His Prague residence contains a huge art collection, which in its day was without equal in Europe. Rumour has it, however, that along with the masterpieces the emperor owned a good deal of worthless junk. He is said to have boasted of owning several

St. Vitus Cathedral

The Interior of St. Vitus Cathedral

Mona Lisas, convinced that each one was genuine. Swedes seized a large part of his collection in 1848, while Emperor Joseph II took some items off to Vienna. Miraculously, however, some works were discovered left discarded in the Deer Moat on the north side of the castle. Following restoration work, they were placed in *Prague Castle Gallery* on the ground floor of the north and west wings of the New Royal Palace. There you can also find paintings by such masters as Titian, Veronese and Rubens. The gateway to the east wing, in which the President's Office is located, can be entered via the third castle courtyard.

The third courtyard is the site of the monumental Gothic **St. Vitus Cathedral***(3).** As is usual for such structures, it took centuries to build. It isn't the oldest religious building in the castle complex, however. By the cathedral are the remains of two separate older structures, where a Romanesque rotunda from the 10th century and the 11th century Roman basilica once stood. The cathedral we see today was begun in 1344 during the reign of John of Luxembourg. The first architect called in was Matthew of Arras (France). His successor Petr Parléř of Gmund, however, was far more adventurous in his plans. It was thanks to him that the cathedral became an architectural

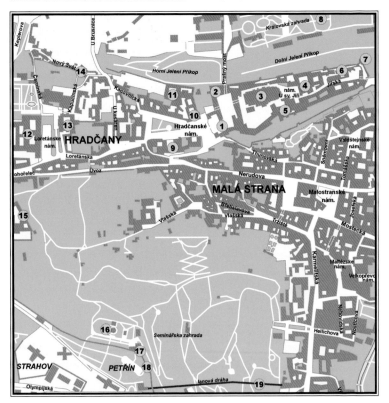

wonder, in many ways ahead of its time. Additions in the 19th century, however, changed the outline of the cathedral considerably. Originally it only had one tower and its composition was more varied. The original tower is the Renaissance Bell-tower with its baroque roof almost 100 metres from the ground. In 1873, major reconstruction work began, which made the cathedral more uniformly neo-Gothic. At the same time, it was extended with two identical neo-Gothic western towers. The most highly appreciated part of the cathedral's exterior is found on the southern side, to the right of the Renaissance Bell-tower. The southern entrance to the cathedral, now no longer in use, is decorated with a superb gothic Golden Gate mosaic, which dates back to the time of Charles IV. Venetian craftsmen depicted a scene of the Last Judgement, considered to be the greatest work of its kind north of the Alps.

The cathedral with its three naves is 124m long and 60m wide. The most valued part of the interior is at the heart of the entire structure – The Chapel of St. Wenceslas, where the saint of the same name was laid to rest. Its walls of mainly gold are covered with Gothic murals and 1,345 jaspers and amethysts. The chapel was built on the very same spot of the apse of a now-vanished Romanesque rotunda, where the most important Bohemian saint was originally buried. On the northern door of the chapel is a bronze knocker, which Wenceslas is supposed to have grasped at when he was treacherously murdered at his brother's castle in Stará Boleslav. Above the saint's final place of rest is the Coronation Chamber, containing the priceless Czech Crown Jewels. Their value is said to exceed that of the entire cathedral. Seven locks protect the entrance to the chamber, which can only be opened by seven key bearers. The keys are in the possession of the Czech president, the prime minister, the archbishop of Prague, the chairman of the Senate, the chairman of the Lower House, the prior of the Metropolitan Chapter House and the mayor of Prague. The Crown Jewels are taken out of the Coronation Chamber only on very special occasions. In the 20th century this only happened nine times. The Crown Jewels must be guarded not only for their great value, but also because they mustn't fall into the wrong hands. Legend has it that when St. Wenceslas's Crown is placed on the head of the unworthy they will meet an untimely fate. The last victim of the curse was the Nazi Reich Protector Reinhard Heydrich during WWII, who was assassinated seven months after he tried on the crown.

Other treasures are hidden in the cathedral's crypt, where the remains of many Bohemian princes and kings are buried, including Charles IV. The crypt contains the bones of the Premyslids and Luxembourgs. The Royal Mausoleum by the high altar, however, belongs to the Hapsburgs. It is the final resting-place of Emperor Ferdinand I, his wife Anna Jagellon and son Emperor Maximilian II. The

View from the Renaissance Belltower

choir stalls, mausoleum and high altar are covered by one of the oldest latticed vaults in Europe. This was Master Petr Parler's greatest achievement. The choir is lined by a row of chapels filled with valuable works of art. One of the most valued is the Chapel of St Jan Nepomucký, which contains the remains of St. Vojtech. Several new elements were fitted in to the original architecture of the cathedral. A nice example is the glass window on the north side of the cathedral nave, the work of art nouveau master Alfons Mucha.

Next to St. Vitus Cathedral is the **House of the New Priory,**** which itself contains the Romanesque Bishop's Palace. The nearby granite **memorial Obelisk*** was erected in 1928 in honour of the victims of the First World War. The sculpture of St. George on horseback is a replica of the original from 1373, which now stands in the National Gallery.

The Basilica of St. George***(4) is, apart from its Baroque facade, a superb example of the Romanesque style. It was built in the 10th century, has two massive towers and an austere interior. Added on later was the Benedictine Convent, the oldest in the Czech Republic. Prince Boleslav II founded the convent in 973, and in front of the monastery are statues of the royal family. The first Abbess was Boleslav's sister Mlada. King Charles IV later gave the abbesses of the convent the honour of crowning the Bohemian kings. At the beginning of the 13th century St. Agnes of Bohemia became the abbess. It was at this time that the tiered Chapel of St. Ludmila was built on to the side of the choir lofts. The former convent now

a group of Protestants. The two Imperial officials fell 15 metres, but survived by landing on a pile of rubbish. This incident resounded around Europe just like the shots fired at Archduke Ferdinand in 1914. The defenestration led to the start of the Thirty Years War.

Jiřská Street, in the eastern part of Prague Castle, is not only the route used to get to Golden Alley, but also the one taken to the Black Tower. Past the gate we come to the romantic **Old Castle Steps,** mentioned in the old Bohemian ballads. These can take us to Klárov and the *Malostranská* metro station. The best time to experience the magic of this small corner of Prague is in the early morning, when the steps aren't crowded with tourists or

Golden Lane (6)

No visitor to Prague Castle should miss Golden Lane, on the northwest side of the castle complex. The smallest street in Prague is lined with miniature houses, which produce a strange effect among the monumental buildings all around them. They are mistakenly thought to be the dwellings of alchemists, attached to the court of Emperor Rudolf II. The inhabitants of Golden Lane did in fact serve Rudolf, but were engaged in something much more mundane – they were his castle gunners. Later the street was taken over by goldsmiths, which probably led to the story of the alchemists. The skilful hands of the goldsmiths and jewellers didn't turn stone into gold, but did turn gold into beautiful objects.

Golden Lane

contains collections of Czech Baroque belonging to the National Gallery, where visitors can get a vivid impression of the works of the best Czech painters and sculptors of the 16th-18th centuries.

The princes, kings, emperors and governors ruled over the Czechs and sometimes also other nations of Central Europe from behind the walls of the **Royal Palace***(5).** The building of this Romanesque palace began in 1135 at the order of King Sobeslav I, and later underwent various reconstruction projects. The most highly-valued part of the palace is the throne of the Bohemian kings in Vladislav Hall, which was created at the end of the 15th century, when three smaller halls were joined together to form the largest unsupported royal hall in Prague. The late-Gothic hall, topped with its cylindrical arches, was used on special occasions. It was even the scene of jousting, with the riders able to enter the hall via the equestrian staircase without dismounting. On May 23, 1618, the hall known as the Bohemian Chancellery was the scene of a former renowned Czech pastime, known as defenestration, when two Catholic governors were helped out of the windows by

full of the cries of souvenir sellers. From the northern side, the castle ramparts tower high above the Deer Moat. The easterly-most tower is called **Daliborka*(7).** In the past it served as a prison. Its first inmate in 1498 was a young knight called Dalibor of Kozojedy. He was imprisoned for hiding serfs who had fled from a neighbouring estate. His sad story was put to music by Bedřich Smetana in the opera of the same name. Dalibor spent the time waiting for his execution by playing the fiddle. He played so well that he attracted crowds of people, who as a sign of their appreciation gave him food and drink in a basket let down on a length of rope.

The **Royal Garden**(8)** to the north of the castle was laid out on the orders of Hapsburg ruler Ferdinand I, supposedly to delight his beloved wife Anne. The Emperor's personal doctor and botanist

The Golden Gate

Pietro A. Mattioli brought tulip bulbs – previously unknown in Europe – from Turkey. These flowers later spread from Prague to the rest of the continent, including, of course, to the Netherlands. Among the various buildings in the Royal Garden, the Royal Summer House built in 1556 deserves particular attention. This superbly delicate structure, also known as the **Belveder**, is among the most beautiful Renaissance buildings outside Italy. Next to the Summer House is the Singing Fountain from 1564. It got its name from the sound of the water falling on the metal tank, but

The Singing Fountain

The Czech Crown Jewels

The Czech Crown Jewels consist of the crown, orb, sceptre and vestments. The royal crown is known as the Crown of St. Wenceslas, even though it was made for Charles IV, who first wore it on September 2, 1347. The crown, made of pure gold, weighs 2.358 kilos, and is decorated with 96 precious stones and 20 pearls. The jewels include sapphires, spinels, emeralds and one rubelite. Some of the gems are among the largest in the world. The gold cross on the top of the crown contains a thorn, which is supposed to come from the crown of thorns worn by Christ. The royal orb and sceptre were made for Emperor Ferdinand I between 1532-1534. The orb, made from 18-carat gold and weighing 780 grams, holds six spinels, eight sapphires and 31 pearls. It is embossed with biblical scenes from the life of Adam and King David. The sceptre is also made of gold. It is 67cm long, and weighs 1.013 kilos. It also contains mainly pearls. The coronation vestments include an ermine robe with woven gold, a stole, a belt, and a so-called maniple – a narrow embroidered band worn hanging from the left arm. The robe is 3.12 metres wide and 2.36 metres long. It was first used for the coronation of Ferdinand II in 1617. Also used at coronations were the St. Wenceslas sword and the golden cross, which supposedly contains objects from Christ's passion (wood from the cross, a part of the sponge that was dipped in vinegar and rope).

The Equestrian Steps in the Royal Palace

Prague Castle from the Vltava river

Hradčany Square

the story goes that the singing comes from a cursed nymph trapped inside the metal.

Hradčany

Castle Guard

In the past, Hradčany was one of a number of independent towns that eventually formed today's Prague. The busiest area in this quarter of the city is Hradčany Square, laid out in front of the west entrance to Prague Castle. It was once full of market traders, but is now thronged with tourists. Most people gather on the southern side, in order to watch the ostentatious changing of the Castle Guard.

The palaces of nobles, who wanted to live as close to the ruling court as possible, surround Hradčany Square. Only a small part of the square is open – in the south-eastern corner, where a terrace looks out on one of the most beautiful views in Prague. The **Schwarzenberg Palace**(9)** can easily be recognised by its richly decorated sgraffito facade. It was built in the 16th century by an Italian architect for a nobleman from Lobkovice, who wasn't able to enjoy it long, as it was taken away from him when he incurred the displeasure of Rudolf II. The Schwarzenburg family bought it in 1719. The presence of the **Archbishop's Palace**(10)** on the other side of the square reflects the political balance of power in the country after the fateful Battle of White Mountain. The head of the Catholic Church in the Czech lands needed to be close to the ruling court and the governor's office. Behind the palace, which is still used by the archbishop today, is the **Šternberk Palace**(11)**, which dates from 1679. For almost two centuries it was a centre for the arts. Count František J. Šternberk, founder of the *Czech National Society of Friends of the Arts*, persuaded his fellow

The Castle Guard

The Prague Castle Guard dates back to 1918, when it was set up for the return of the first President of Czechoslovakia Tomas G. Masaryk from exile. When the Czech lands were occupied in March 1939, the Castle Guard was taken over by the Germans. What the Fascists failed to do, the Communists accomplished after WWII. Communist president Klement Gottwald disbanded the Castle Guard and had it replaced by the National Security Corps. The Velvet Revolution of 1989, however, restored the Castle Guard to its pre-war prestige. During the visit of former German president Richard von Weizsäker the Guard first appeared in its ceremonial uniform, which was conceived by the world-famous film-costume designer and Oscar winner Theodor Pištěk. The first set of costumes was made at the Adam Fashion Salon in Prague. The Castle Guard is now a thousand strong. Besides Prague Castle, it also guards the president's residence in Lány.

The Archbishop's Palace

noblemen at the beginning of the 18th century to donate part of their private collections to a public exhibition at his Hradčany residence. In 1811 it was transformed into the forerunner of today's *National Gallery*. Today, the palace houses a permanent exhibition: *European Art from Antiquity to the End of the Baroque Period*. Here you can find works produced by world-renowned masters, such as Rembrandt, El Greco, Rubens, Goya and Van Dyck. The most valuable piece is the large *Feast of the Rose Garlands*, painted by Albrecht Durer in 1506.

The Prague Sun

The Loreta

Loreta Square, in the western part of Hradčany, is squeezed between two domineering buildings. On the west is **Černín Palace*(12).** A wide building with a 150-metre-long facade, it reflects the megalomania of its former owner. Count Jan Černin of Chudenice wanted the imposing size of his palace to counter-balance Prague Castle. On the eastern side of Loreta Square is the Prague **Loreta**(13)**.

Begun in 1621, this most important place of pilgrimage in Prague is the greatest work of the Baroque period in the Czech Republic. The centrepiece of the complex is the Loreta Chapel, built in the middle of the inner courtyard. This, like other buildings of its type, is an almost exact replica of the so-called original House of the Virgin Mary in Nazareth, which was brought from the Holy Land to the Italian city Loreta. The prominent feature of the Prague Loreta is an elegant Baroque tower with its famous chimes. Every hour throughout the day, the Magnificat is rung out by 27 bells of various sizes, which are connected to a special keyboard. The Loreta also contains the renowned *Loreta Treasure*. The most valuable piece in this collection of religious works is the *Prague Sun* monstrance from 1699, inlaid with 6,222 diamonds.

In the northeast corner of Hradčany is a beautiful little street called **Nový svět*(14)** (New World). Its small houses are unusual and picturesque. It is as if time has stood still. In 1600, one of these narrow houses called Golden Noh's was the home of the famous astronomer Tycho de Brahe. One of his colleagues was Johannes Kepler, who formulated the famous law of the movement of planets on elliptical orbits.

Strahov Monastery

Strahov and Petřín

To the southwest of Hradčany is the quarter known as Strahov, famous thanks to its ancient monastery and giant stadium. **Strahov Monastery**(15)** is one of the oldest in the Czech Republic. Despite its Baroque facade, it dates back to 1140. Its founder was King Vladislav II. Originally it was designed to be the final resting place of the Czech rulers, but in fact only Vladislav himself and his wife Gertrude are buried there. The original Assumption of the Virgin Mary Basilica has had to withstand serious fires and wars. In the chapel adjoining the northern side nave are the remains of St. Norbert, the founder of the Premonstrate Order. This order came here in 1627 from the German city Magdeburg, which had been captured by Swedish troops. Mozart played its large Baroque organ in 1787 and his improvised piece was transcribed by organist Norbert Lehman and later published as the *Strahov Variation*. In 1950, the monastery was designated a *Monument of National Literature* with the function of mapping out the history of Czech literature. The monastery's relationship with books and literature began at the end of the 18th century with the building of the famous Strahov Library, a free-standing building that housed more than 900,000 volumes. The most beautiful interiors in the Strahov Monastery are found in two richly decorated rooms – the Philosophy Hall and the Theology Hall.

A favourite destination for the people of Prague is **Petřín**. From the Vltava river it looks like a wooded hill, but in fact it forms the edge of a wide plain, on which stand the Strahov stadium and student dormitories. A really good conception of this part of Prague can only be gained once you have climbed the 299 steps of the **Petřín Watchtower*(16)**. Almost right

The Basilica of the Assumption

The Theology Hall

Hradčany from the Petřín Watchtower

Prague's Eiffel Tower

The Petrin Watchtower is a miniature version of the famous Eiffel Tower in Paris. It is only around one fifth the height of the original, but as it stands on an elevated spot, its 60 metres gives you a fantastic view over the whole of Prague. Apart from their appearance, the two towers also have the same 'birth certificate'. The Eiffel Tower was built as an exhibit for the World Exhibition in Paris in 1889, while the Petrin tower owes its existence to the Jubilee Exhibition that took place in Prague two years later. At the same time, a Hall of Mirrors was built, including a panorama of the battle between the citizens of Prague and the Swedes in 1648.

The Church of St. Vavrinec

beneath the steel tower is the 18th century Baroque **Church of St. Lawrence*(17).** The wall paintings in the sacristan depict the legend of how an earlier church was built on this site by St. Vojtech and the pious Prince Boleslav II. Archaeological research has confirmed the existence of an old Romanesque religious building below the church. In fact, traces of an even earlier pagan temple were discovered. Along the eastern part of Petřín runs the **Hunger Wall*(18),** which emerged as far back as the time of Charles IV, in order to protect the Lesser Town and Hradčany. Its name comes from the fact that it was supposedly built to provide work for the poor and prevent them from starving, an early social project. It is possible to get to Petřín on the **Petřín Funicular Railway*(19),** which has been running from the Újezd station since 1891. From the Nebozízek station, loca-

ted halfway up, you get a good view over Hradčany. A very pleasant walk is the route to Petřín from Strahov Monastery, which goes through orchards that are especially pretty in May. The view of Prague Castle over the orchard's blossoming trees is not one that is quickly forgotten.One of Prague's most beautiful streets, full of historical palaces and the houses of wealthy citizens, is **Nerudova Street.** By looking at

THE LESSER TOWN

The southern slopes below Hradčany are red as a result of the roofs of its houses, which seem to merge into a great river of red flowing into the Vltava. This is one of the city's most picturesque parts – the Lesser Town, which emerged as Prague's second town. It was founded in 1257 by King Přemysl Otakar II. At first it was known as Prague's New Town, until this name was given to another part of the city founded by Charles IV in 1348. This part of Prague has long had a residential character, as nobles wanted to live near Prague Castle and built their palaces here. Today's Lesser Town not only links the Old Town with Prague Castle, it also has something special to offer visitors – splendid palaces, superb gardens and marvellous churches, as well as the odd romantic little corner.

The Lesser Town

Nerudova Street

the signs you can find out what the houses are called. For example, there is the House of the Three Fiddles, The Red Eagle House and the White Swan House. The famous Czech writer and journalist Jan Neruda (1834-1891), after whom the street is named, lived in the **House of the Two Suns*(20)** for

The Church of St. Nicholas

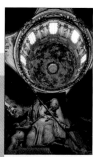

The Dome

12 years. Closely observing life in the Lesser Town, he painted a rich picture of its inhabitants in his famous *Lesser-Town Stories*.

Nerudova Street runs down into the Lesser Town Square, which is lined with palaces built in various styles. A good example of a Renaissance-style nobleman's residence with Baroque reconstruction work is the **Smiřický Palace**(21)** on the northern side. The architect of the neighbouring **Šternberk Palace**(22)** made it clear that the palace was fashioned out of two Renaissance houses. Both the Imperial and Classical styles are evident in the **Liechtenstein Palace**(23)** on the western side of the square. In the 17th century this palace belonged to Governor Charles Liechtenstein, who, acting as an extended arm of the Hapsburgs, had the dubious distinction of overseeing the severe repression of Protestants after the Battle of White Mountain. The **Kaiserstein Palace*(24)** on the eastern side of the square, and the **Hartigov Palace*(25)** on the southern side are both beautiful examples of the Baroque style.

It would be difficult to find a more artistically rich and triumphant accomplishment of the Baroque style than the **Church of St. Nicholas***(26).** Its enormous dimensions fill the centre of the Lesser Town Square, which as a result does not seem like a square at all. Construction of the church began in 1703, and the building work continued for more than half a century. The main architects – the father-and-son team the Dienzenhofs – were not around to see its completion in 1761. The church is easily recognisable from the outside by its tall tower topped by an oval-shaped dome. Slightly higher is

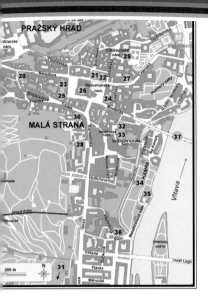

The Infant Jesus of Prague

the neighbouring square-shaped tower, which actually doesn't belong to the church. This tower, which is accessible to the public, was built for defensive purposes with money collected from Lesser Town citizens. The interior of the Church of St. Nicholas is filled with art of the highest quality. It contains many Baroque frescos, statues, altar paintings, stucco – all by the greatest masters of their time, such as Karel Škréta, Ignác F. Platzer, the Prachners and Fridrich Kohl. Probably the most beautiful part of the interior is the illusive fresco painted in the dome by František X. Palka. The church's acoustics have been tested by many musical greats, including W.A. Mozart. To this day the church is used for serious music concerts. Another great example of the best that the Baroque style has to offer is the **Church of St. Thomas*(27)**, with its valuable frescos painted by Václav V. Reiner in 1728-1730. On Karmelitánska (or Carmelitan) Street is the **Church of the Virgin Mary Victorious***(28)** from the beginning of the 17th century. This is worth a visit, not least because it contains the famous *Infant Jesus of Prague* statue.

The Lesser Town's charm is enhanced by its splendid historical gardens. One of the most beautiful of these is attached to the **Valdštejn Palace***(29)**. This was built in the 17th century for the Commander of the Imperial Army Albert of Valdštejn (1581-1634), and was the first Baroque-style secular building to appear in Bohemia. The flamboyance and luxury of the palace gardens reflect the ambition of their original owner, who wanted it to stand out with its splendid statues, its 30-metre-high salla terrena, and its charming backdrop – Prague Castle. Other gardens can be found behind the palace on the opposite side of Valdštejnska Street. These are terraced, as they are found on a steep slope beneath the walls of Prague Castle. It is difficult to say which of the six palace gardens are the most beautiful, but you can decide for

The Infant Jesus of Prague

Prague has one of the greatest church symbols in Central Europe. The Catholic Church usually refers to this miniature wax statue by the Italian name of 'Bambini di Praga', although it actually originally came from Spain, where it is known as 'Niño Jesús de Praga'. It was placed in the Lesser Town church in 1628 after being transported to Prague by Marie Manrique, wife of a Bohemian aristocrat called Vratislav of Pernštejn. Marie's daughter Polyxéna later donated it to the Carmelite monks. The statue is 45cm tall, and is considered to have miraculous healing powers. It is credited with protecting Prague from plague and wartime suffering. There are many copies of the statue found throughout the world, including, for example, in the city of Cartago in distant Costa Rica. Missionaries took another replica to the Philippines. The faithful have given many small presents to the statue, mainly clothes. It has a wardrobe that any princess would be proud of. Empress Maria Theresia herself made a small velvet dress for the statue, and a garment bearing a dragon was sent from Vietnam. The statue's clothes are changed several times a year according to the church calendar.

yourself, as all of them are open to the public. There are two palace gardens on the slopes of Petřín hill. A wonderful view of the main features of the Lesser Town can be gained from the charming garden behind **Vrtbovský Palace**(30)**. This also contains a salla terrena adorned by Václav V. Reiner's superb frescos. The Kinský Garden above the Impe-

Kinský Summerhouse

The John Lennon Wall

rial-style **Kinský Summerhouse*(31)** (early 19th century) is found on the boundary between the Lesser Town and Smíchov suburb. It is more like an English park than a garden. Its romantic natural surroundings include a small lake, a waterfall and miniature sculptures. In 1905, the summerhouse was used to house the National Museum's folklore exhibition. Part of this exhibition was supposed to be a recreation of a traditional village in the gardens. The only part of this village that actually went on show was a wooden church brought from Western Ukraine.

The names of two small squares near the Charles Bridge indicate that this part of the Lesser Town is closely connected to an order of Maltese knights. Members of the Order of the Knights of St. John from the Mediterranean island of Malta founded the oldest church in the Lesser Town – the 12th-century **Church of the Virgin Mary beneath the**

The John Lennon Wall

Shortly after a malicious assassin shot dead the legendary ex-Beatle John Lennon in 1980, a portrait of Lennon appeared on a wall in the Grand Prior's Garden. The wall was soon covered with other creative works and various quotes from the great musician, who had been a leader of the peace movement. The place acquired a cult status, with not only fans of Lennon meeting here, but also opponents of the Communist regime. Although the wall was a big thorn in the side of the Communists, it survived, and you can still go and read the countless quotes and messages today, including the piece that John Lennon's widow Yoko Ono wrote in 2003.

Chain*(32). This church is part of a monastery, which also includes the **Baroque Grand Prior's Palace*(33)**. This was the residence of the grand prior, the second-most senior member of the Order of the Knights of St. John, who represented the head of the order – the grand master – in Bohemia.

The most romantic spot in the Lesser Town is on **Kampa Island**(34)**. The quiet seclusion near the Čertovka millstream is evocative of Venice. In the centre of Kampa is a small square, which was once the site of the lively ceramics market. They still sell ceramics here today in the form of popular souvenirs. The wheel of the Huť watermill, built by the Order of the Knights of St. John in the 13ᵗʰ century, nicely complements the historical surroundings. If the mill could talk, it could give a dramatic account of the great floods that have hit this low-lying island over the centuries. The last time the Čertovka overflowed its banks was in the memorable floods of 2002, in which the **Sova's Mills*(35)** suffered the most serious damage. These mills, which had stood on this spot since the Middle Ages, had been converted into art galleries, which among other works included a collection of paintings by leading

Kampa Island in the 19ᵗʰ century

The Huť Water Mill

The Čertovka stream

Czech artist František Kupka (1871-1957). One of the paintings is on show outside. At the end of the embankment, you can't miss the giant wooden chair by Magdaléna Jetelová. Near to the spot where the Čertovka flows back into the Vltava river is the small 13ᵗʰ century **Church of St. John at the Laundry*(36)**. It got its unusual name because in 1784 Emperor Joseph II ordered it to be converted into a laundry. It was re-consecrated in 1935. Clothes were being washed and bleached here on the banks of the Čertovka and Vltava back in the Middle Ages. Many of the washerwomen were renowned beauties. Rudolf II's official court launderer also worked here.

The Charles Bridge***(37)

Charles Bridge is located in an ideal position, at the obvious linking point between Old Town and Lesser Town. It is the oldest bridge in Prague still standing, but not the first. There was an earlier wooden bridge slightly further downstream. The first stone bridge – named after Judith, wife of Vladislav I – was built in 1172. Judith's Bridge stood roughly where the Charles Bridge is now, until it was badly damaged in a flood in 1342. Only a couple of details from it have been preserved. The statue of the 'bearded man' was probably once part of the bridge. When some of the bridge pillars were still in place, they served to measure the level of the river. If the water reached the bearded man's head, the Vltava was in danger of bursting its banks. Another reminder of Judith's Bridge is the relief on the east wall of the Romanesque Judith's Tower, the lower of the Lesser Town's two bridge towers. This relief appeared in 1170, and is the oldest secular piece of art in Prague. The tower was built before the bridge, and was part of the Lesser Town fortifications.

Charles Bridge was begun in 1357, with the foundation stone laid by King Charles IV himself. The king entrusted the building work to the most skilled person he could find – Petr Parléř, builder of St. Vitus Cathedral. His influence can clearly be seen in the Old Town Bridge Tower, which is considered to be one of the finest Gothic structures in Europe. The bridge was built from sandstone blocks. According to a legend, raw eggs and wine were added to the mortar. When not enough eggs could be found in Prague, the king ordered that they be brought in from all over the country. The bridge was completed at the beginning of the 16ᵗʰ century, long after the deaths of its two main creators – Charles IV and Petr Parléř. For a long time it was known as Prague Bridge or Stone Bridge. It was only in 1870 that an old proposal of Czech writer and journalist Karl Havlíček Borovský – that the bridge should be na-

Charles Bridge

Prague Bridges

The Charles Bridge was the only crossing point over the Vltava river in Prague for many years. The second one was built only in 1845, with the grand opening of the Franz I Bridge. This bridge is no longer standing, and was replaced by the Legion Bridge (near the National Theatre). There are now 18 bridges over the Vltava river in Prague. Three of these are made of steel. The most noteworthy of these is the Negrelli Bridge (1850), which connects Karlín with Holešovice. It's interesting not only because it's the longest (1.11km), but also because Alois Negrelli (1799-1858), the engineer responsible for the Suez and Corinth canals, designed it. The newest bridge is the Barrandov from 1978, built at a slant between the districts of Barrandov and Braník, whose dimensions make it the record holder among the Prague bridges. It is only a question of time, however, before it ceases to be the newest.

med after the Father of the Czech Nation Charles IV – was dusted off and accepted.

The Charles Bridge is 516 metres long and 10 metres wide and is supported by 16 pillars. The statues of various saints placed on the bridge appeared gradually. The oldest is the statue of St. Jan Nepomucký from 1683, which stands near the middle of the bridge. This Czech saint often appears on historical bridges, as a traditional defender of towns and villages from floods. One of the bronze reliefs on the plinth depicts the casting of the tortured body of St. Jan Nepomucký into the Vltava. The saint had incurred the wrath of King Wenceslas IV for refusing to reveal a secret entrusted to him by the queen during her confessional. St. Jan Nepomucký was the

Catholic's answer to the reformer Jan Hus, and his cult was used by the Hapsburgs when they were turning the monarchy back into a Catholic one. Other popular statues are those of St. John of Matha, Felix of Valois and St. Ivan. A sculpture produced by Ferdinand M. Brokoff in 1714 became known as 'the Prague Turk', as it depicts a Turk guarding Christian prisoners. The last statues to be added to the bridge were those of St. Cyril and St. Methodius in 1938. Attention should also be paid to the statue of Brunswick the Knight, which stands on one of the bridge's pillars. Brunswick is supposed to have brought the first tamed lion to Bohemia, which led to this powerful animal being adopted as a Czech symbol.

Spotting the Old Town on a map of Prague is not difficult at all. The dense labyrinth of streets and squares with a minimal number of straight lines is clearly bordered by the Vltava river and the wide boulevards that appeared outside the former city walls. Old Town contains a huge number of monuments packed into it. The oldest of these recall the days of old, when this oldest of Prague's historic towns first emerged. The rapidly beating heart of the Old Town is the Old Town Square, and its vital arteries are Celetná Street and Karlova Street. In the past, royal processions followed these routes, now they are filled with crowds of tourists. Only the northern part of this unique historic space has any order to it. It received this in the 19th century when the picturesque Jewish town of Josefov was full of buildings in the Parisian style. Fortunately, providence has preserved the most precious Jewish monuments, which today are among the biggest attractions in the city.

Old-Town Square

In the Old Town

The Old-Town Orloj

A skeleton standing on the upper right signals the beginning of the clock's 'performance'. He rings a bell by pulling on a rope. This is followed by the arrival of the main 'actors' – the twelve apostles. The first to appear is St. Peter and later the other eleven apostles, taking turns to show their faces from two windows. When the final figure leaves the stage, a cock crows, and the clock strikes the hour. The Orloj has other moving figures, each of which is symbolic. The skeleton symbolises the transience of human life. Next to him is the figure of a Turk, who stands for cruelty and treachery. On the left side is a vain figure looking proudly into a mirror, and a miser, who appears in the form of a Jewish moneylender. Another part of the Orloj is the sophisticated mechanism of the astronomical clock. It shows three separate times, the official one, the so-called 'old Czech' and the Babylonian. The superstitious can make predictions from the movement of the heavenly bodies among the signs of the zodiac. The disc below is a calendar with 12 paintings by Josef Mánes, who depicted countryside activities for each month of the year.

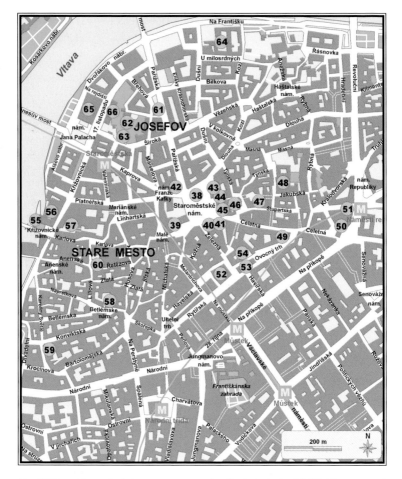

The Old-Town Square is the largest open space in the Old Town, surrounded by narrow and winding streets. As early as the 12th century there were stone-built houses here. The lively marketplace was the scene of many important historical events, often melancholic and tragic. In 1437, the

The Old Town Square

last Hussite leader Jan Roháč Dubé was executed on the square. On June 21, 1621, other political opponents were dealt with. The notorious executioner Mydlář, who for Czechs became synonymous with cruelty, dispatched 27 Czech Protestant leaders of the anti-Hapsburg uprising. The square is also the site of the so-called Prague meridian by which the city's time was calculated. A metal sign showing its position can be found near the **Art Nouveau-style Monument to Jan Hus*(38),** which has been on the square since 1915.

The largest numbers of tourists usually gather in front of the **Old-Town Hall***(39)**. Many turn their gaze on the southern wall of the town hall tower, where every hour the 15th-century Old-Town Orloj, or Astronomical Clock shows what it can do. The Old Town Hall was built like many others as a group of houses for wealthy citizens. Prague was granted the right to its own

The Old Town Hall

Jan Hus Monument

town hall by King John of Luxembourg in 1338. The town hall was gradually extended and improved. Its appearance today is the result of extensive reconstruction work, after German tanks fired on it in 1945. This reconstruction only saved the oldest parts of the severely damaged structure. The newer-style wings on the eastern side were demolished. Some original medieval paintings inside the building were saved. We recommend climbing the Town-Hall Tower to get a nice view over Prague. There's a lift for disabled people.

On the southern side of the Old-Town Square are the narrow burghers' houses, many of which now contain cafés, restaurants, shops and art galleries. The splendid signs help you to guess the names of the houses. **The Golden Unicorn House*(40)** on the corner of Železná Street was a literary salon once visited by Franz Kafka. Over on the left, you can see a fresco painted by Miloláš Aleš on the front of the **Štorchov House*(41)**. On the northern side of the square is the domineering Baroque **Church of St. Nicholas*(42)**, built in 1735 by Kilián Ignác Dienzenhofer. In the dome of the church are paintings from the life of St. Nicholas by Mikoláš Aleš, and of St. Benedict by Kzm D. Asam. The colourful eastern side of the square is the most highly praised. The most noticeable building here is the Rococo **Goltz-Kinský Palace**(43)**, built in 1786. The turreted house on the right has a very old appearance. Reconstruction work on this **Stone Bell House**(44)** in 1980 revealed that behind the masonry hides a Gothic palace, one of the most significant of its kind in Central Europe. The former residents of the house can only be guessed at. Queen Eliška Přemyslovna and her son could have been among them, or King Charles IV. Today, the building is used as the *Prague City Gallery*. Further to the right is another medieval building – the **Tyn School**(45)**, with its well-preserved ribbed arches in the cellar, and its beautiful Renaissance facade.

Eastern Old Town

Tycho de Brahe

Tyn Church Portal

The Church of Our Lady of Tyn(46)**, or simply, the Tyn Church, has been the main church of Prague's Old Town since the Middle Ages. It took a long time to build – from 1350-1511. From 1373, the priest here was St. Jan Nepomucký. It has two redoubtable towers, three naves and three presbyteries. Until the 17th century there was a golden chalice fixed on the central pinnacle that symbolised that the Tyn Church was the stronghold of the Prague Hussites. Beneath the chalice was a sculpture of the 'Hussite King' George of Poděbrady. After the Battle of White Mountain, however, students from the Jesuit school tore down both these symbols. In the free space was placed the Mother of God sculpture we can see today. The halo was made from the melted-down golden chalice. Of particular note is the northern Gothic gate accessible from Tyn Street, clearly the work of architect Petr Parléř. Inside the church are nine famous altarpieces with paintings of foremost baroque masters, including Karel Škréta (1610-1674). The church also contains the remains of Emperor Rudolf II's royal astronomer Tycho de Brahe (1546-1601). Doubts as to whether the tomb with its beautiful stone was really the final resting-place of the famous Dane were dispelled by expert analysis. He was identified by his copper false nose, which had been made to replace his real nose, lost in his youth in a duel.

Behind the Tyn Church is a complex of medieval buildings called the **Ungelt**(47)**. It's also called the Tyn Courtyard, whose name was transferred to the neighbouring church and school. In the old Czech language, the word *tyn* meant something similar to fort or fortification. Its similarity to the English word *town* is no coincidence. By at least the 11th century, there was a royal courtyard here, which was used as a customs house. Merchants coming to the Prague marketplaces had to pay a special tax here, or an *ungelt* (German name for tax). In return they had guaranteed protection, and were allowed to stay here. The Ungelt was used as a customs house until 1774. Today, tourists often visit this successfully restored historical complex. The most noteworthy building is the Renaissance Granov House from the 16th century.

The Church of St. James the Elder**(48) with its impressive dimensions is almost able to compete with the nearby Tyn Church. From the outside its architecture is lost in the

The Ungelt

dense buildings, and the huge nave of the church is what really impresses. The church was built as part of a Minorite monastery founded in 1232. In the 17th century, the medieval building was reconstructed in the Baroque style, while preserving its Gothic proportions. The most noteworthy part of the interior is the Baroque tomb of the Czech Chancellor Jan of Mitrovice, decorated with excellent sculptures by Ferdinand M. Brokoff. The chancellor died in dramatic circumstances. When they placed what they thought was his dead body in the tomb, he 'came back to life'. But he was in a trap, from which there was no way out, and he died a second time in terrible agony. When the tomb was opened several years later, to add the body of another family member, they found the dead body of the chancellor with a horrific grimace on his face.

Eastward from the Old-Town Square leads **Celetná Street,** which has been made into a pedestrian zone. Many tourists walk down here because it is on the route of the so-called *Royal Way,* used in the past for coronation processions. The name of the street comes from a plaited bread roll, which was called a *calt.* Among the historical buildings on the street with their house-names displayed, the modern-looking **House of the Black Madonna**(49)** stands out. Its name comes from the Black Madonna with Child statue on a stone that juts out at the level of the first floor. Josef Gočál built the house in 1911-12. It's a jewel of Czech and world cubism, and the oldest building in this style – made famous by Pablo Picasso. It's interesting to note that the best examples of this kind of architecture are found in the Czech Republic.

On Republic Square stand two completely separate buildings side by side. Although they are dif-

The Royal Way

Today, the Royal Way is the most popular tourist route in Prague, passing by practically all the most important monuments in the city. In the past it had the distinction of connecting two important royal residences – The King's Palace, standing on the site of today's Municipal House, and Prague Castle. The Royal Way was also used by coronation processions. The first monarch to use it in this way was King George of Poděbrady. In 1743, the coronation procession of the Empress Maria Theresia passed this way with a great deal of pomp. The last ruler to use the Royal Way was Ferdinand V in 1836. Further on is the winding Karlova Street, which leads to the Charles Bridge. Beyond the Vltava river is Bridge Street, which runs into Lesser-Town Square. The final section of the Royal Way leads upwards via Nerudova Street to Prague Castle.

The Black Madonna House

The Municipal House

The Powder Gate

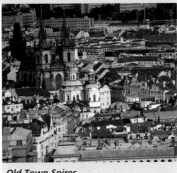

Old Town Spires

can climb up the tower for a great view of the city. To the right is **Municipal House**(51),** whose architecture is completely different. This is the most beautiful Art Nouveau building in Prague. It was here that the medieval Royal Palace once stood. This was in such a poor state by 1903, however, that it had to be demolished. The Municipal House, built in its place in 1905, now has pride of place in Prague. Its unique outer decoration in the Art Nouveau style is Karel Špilar's monumental semi-circular mosaic, called *Homage to Prague.* The interior contains the beautiful works of Max Švabinský, Alfons Mucha, Mikoláš Aleš, and other Czech artists. It was in the Smetana Concert Hall that the first Czechoslovak republic was declared on October 28, 1918. During the Velvet Revolution in November 1989, the Municipal House was the site of the first meeting between the outgoing Communist government and the newly formed Citizen's Forum. Fortunately, Smetana Hall is more an artistic space than a political one. During the international *Prague Spring* music festival concerts are put on here.

ferent in age, style and colour, they create one of Prague's most beautiful scenes. On the left is the much older **Powder Gate**(50),** whose predecessor stood here from the 13th century. It formed the entrance into the walled city for merchants arriving from the town of Kutná Hora. It is also called the Hill Gate. King Vladislav Jagellon, who left the building work to Matěj Rejsk from Prostějov, laid the foundation stone in 1475. Influenced by Petr Parléř, he fashioned the structure on the Old Town Bridge Tower. The Powder Gate is so called because gunpowder was kept here. You

The Havel Street Market

Havel's Town

The Estates Theatre

The Coal Market

The Karolinum

Havel's Town is the name of the southern part of Prague's Old Town between the Coal and Fruit Markets. It emerged in the 13th century, filling an empty space between the oldest buildings of Romanesque Prague and the southern walls. Today, it is a busy link between two of the largest open spaces in Prague – the Old-Town Square and Wenceslas Square. At the eastern end of Havel Street, with its lively fruit market, is the 13th century **Church of St. Havel*(52)**, which is one of the Old Town's four parish churches. Close by is the classical building of the **Estates Theatre*(53),** which is also known as Tyl Theatre. It was begun in 1783 on the orders of Count František A. Nostic. Its main claim to fame is that it is where the world premiere of Mozart's opera *Don Giovanni* took place on October 29, 1797, with Mozart himself conducting the orchestra. The opera soon conquered the world. Another great premiere took place here on December 21, 1834 – a major event for the Czech nation. The song *Where's My Home?*, which in 1918 became the Czech national anthem, was first performed here on that date during a play written by Josef Kajetán Tyl (1808-1856) called *Fidlovačka*.

Jutting out into the narrow street at the side of the Estates Theatre is a Gothic bay window. This belongs to the oldest part of a complex of buildings belonging to Charles University known as the **Karolinum***(54).** This is found at the heart of Central Europe's oldest university, founded by Charles IV in 1348. The university was already in existence, but it didn't have a proper home. It wasn't until 1383 that it was granted the Gothic Rotler House by Vaclav IV. This was gradually expanded into today's predominantly Baroque Karolinum. Within it are oldest parts with their original Gothic arches, but also the modern entrance built after WWII. In the courtyard is a statue of Jan Hus, who was rector of the university for two separate periods. In the Karolinum's University Hall the first public debate took place in which Hus and his friend Jerome of Prague attacked the Catholic Church's practice of selling indulgences. In 1420, university professors wrote *The Four Articles of Prague*, which contains the reformist demands of the Hussite movement.

The Western Old Town

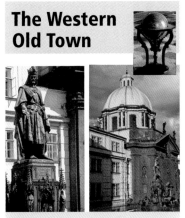

Knights of the Cross Square

The narrow and winding **Karlova (Charles) Street** is among the busiest in the city, because it joins the Old Town Square with the Charles Bridge, and forms part of the Royal Way. Its winding course makes it obvious that it emerged in the 12th century during the busiest period of Romanesque building work. At its western end, Karlova Street opens out on to the unusually picturesque **Knights of the Cross Square** insensitively crossed by busy roads. The large neo-Gothic **Charles IV Monument*(55)** on the square reminds passers-by who deserves the credit for Charles Bridge, which they are just about to cross. The monument was unveiled in 1848 to commemorate the 500th anniversary of the founding of Charles University. Next to the monument is **the Church of St. Francis the Seraph*(56)**, built between 1679-85. It is part of an old monastery that was founded in 1252. The monastery belonged to the Knights of the Cross (with red star), the only genuinely Czech order of monks, who collected donations and a toll for the use of the bridge. From 1561-1694, the well-respected Knights of the Cross elected the archbishop of Prague. Another church located on the square is the Baroque St. Saviour's Church, which looks out over the bridge. This church is part of a complex of historical buildings called the **Clementinum**(57)**, which includes another two churches – the so-called Vlašská Chapel and the Church of St. Clement. In 1556, Emperor Ferdinand I invited the Jesuits to Prague, and gave them the former Dominican monastery of St Clement's near Charles Bridge. The Jesuits gradually built up a spiritual, cultural and educational centre aimed at turning the Czechs back to the Catholic Church. The complex also included a boarding school. Later, as a university, it became a serious rival to Charles University. Science was also successfully developed at the Clementinum. The Astronomical Tower (open to the public as a lookout point) in its day contained a well-equipped observatory. From 1775 regular meteorological observations began which have lasted to this day. The Clementinum has the longest record of temperature and atmospheric pressure measurements in the Czech Republic.

The robust and towerless **Bethlehem Chapel**(58)** was built between 1391-1394 due to a lack of spacious halls suitable for preaching. The chapel, which could hold as many as 3,000 people, was used for preaching by the legendary Jan Hus. For ten years he shared his thoughts with the people, leading to the emergence of the Hussite movement. Influenced by the teachings of English religious reformer John Wycliffe, Hus spoke from the Bethlehem Chapel pulpit about the pressing need to bring about change in both the Church and society. The Pope was displeased mainly by his criticism of the selling of indulgences, which were the source of a large part of his income. For this reason he declared Hus anathema. Hus decided to leave Prague and continue preaching in the southern Bohemian countryside. Today's Bethlehem Chapel is a faithful copy of the one that stood in Hus's time but was demolished in 1786.

Church of St. Salvátor

View of the Clementinum from The Bridge Tower

The Clementinum Library

The Bethlehem Chapel

The St. Cross Chapel

The old **Rotunda of Saint Cross the Lesser**(59)** on Konvitská Street is one of the oldest Romanesque buildings in Prague. It contains the precious 14th century Gothic fresco *The Adoration of the Magi*. Today it is the parish church of the Old-Catholic Church. Anther higher-valued Romanesque structure is the **House of the Gentlemen of Kunštát**(60)** on Řeťezová Street. Inside the house was discovered a noteworthy well-preserved vault of a Romanesque courtyard from the 12th century. Originally it was part of the ground-floor level of a palace. In 1451 George of Poděbrady moved into the palace and lived there until he was elected as Czech king in 1458.

Pařížská Street from the Old Town Hall Tower

Josefov

Pařížská Street from Letná

Once the autonomous Jewish Prague town, Josefov, was merged with the Old Town. Today it forms its northern part. As early as 1091 there were two Jewish settlements to the north of the Old Town Square. They gradually merged and formed a closed town – a ghetto with its own autonomous authority, synagogues and education system. Its inhabitants were long subject to attacks and discrimination. During the reign of

Joseph II, the status of Prague's Jews improved, and the Jews named their town after Joseph as a sign of gratitude, but the people of Josefov continued to be victims of pogroms and forced evictions. The severest blows, however, came in more recent times. While the great amount of building work in the 19th century produced an area of picturesque streets and squares, the holocaust during WWII deprived it of its inhabitants. Only a few of Prague's Jews returned after the war to the town where their forefathers had lived for almost nine centuries.

Prague is not called 'Little Paris' for nothing. The extensive building work at the end of the 19th and beginning of the 20th centuries in Josefov were modelled on the French capital. A nice example is the elegant **Pařížská (Paris) Street.** Its construction produced a valuable architectural area consisting of impressive apartment blocks bearing the stamp of the developed Art Nouveau and various other styles that were fashionable at the time.

Fortunately, the builders of Josefov had the foresight to preserve the most valuable Jewish monuments. Today, these act as one of the biggest tourist magnets in Prague, and the town has made a decent living out of tourism. Crowds of tourists, not only Jewish, walk from one monument to another, as they are not all concentrated in the same area. The most noteworthy monument is the so-called **Old-New Synagogue***(61),** which is the oldest in the whole of Europe. It was built some time after 1270 as one of the first Gothic buildings in Prague. It was and still is the main centre of Prague's Jewish community. According to one of the synagogue legends, it was brought to Prague from Jerusalem by an angel.

The Old Jewish Cemetery

A slightly more realistic rendition has it that it was built from stones brought from the ruins of the Jerusalem temple. The synagogue is remarkable for the 14th-century Jewish banner. King Charles IV gave the Jews the right to carry it in 1354. The banner is valuable because it bears the first ever depiction of the six-pointed Star of David, which spread from Prague throughout the world as the classic Jewish symbol, also chosen by the state of Israel and included on the national flag. Inside the synagogue is the rare rabbi's throne, on which the most famous

Prague Rabbi Löw sat from 1597-1609. The grave of this celebrated Jewish teacher can be found in the **Old Jewish Cemetery**(62),** which is less than a hectare in size, and couldn't expand any further, making it necessary to dig multi-level graves. In just under 350 years it was necessary to bury around a hundred thousand people here in 12 levels with the oldest grave – that of Rabbi Avigdor Kary – dating back to 1439. The last person to be buried here was Moses Beck in 1787. Today, around 12,000 graves remain. Packed in close together they resemble a sto-

The Old-New Synagogue

The Pinkas Synagogue

ne forest. Next to the cemetery is the **Pinkas Synagogue**(63)**, which is the second oldest, built in 1479. It is named after the rabbi who founded it. After WWII it was turned into a memorial to the victims of Nazism. On its walls are written the names of all the Jews of the Czech lands who died in Nazi concentration camps. This longest inscription in the world contains 77,297 names.

In the second half of the 19th century and during the 20th century, the right bank of the Vltava river between the Charles and Štefánik Bridges was gradually filled with many representative buildings. One of the small monuments that have fortunately escaped the building frenzy is the **Monastery of St. Agnes of Bohemia**(64)**. This was built in 1230 by Sister Agnes the Premyslid (1211-1282) – daughter of the powerful King Přemysl Otakar I, and sister of King Wenceslas I – who had suitors from some of the most notable European ruling families. Once betrothed to the promising Emperor Frederick II and the English King Henry VII, Agnes chose God instead. Following the death of her father she decided to take St. Clare and St. Francis of Assisi as her role models and entered a monastery. She became the first Abbess of the Order of St. Clare, for which she founded a monastery on the banks of the Vltava. The Order of St. Clare was a female offshoot of the Franciscans, which is why her Prague monastery acquired the nickname of the 'Bohemian Assisi'. Agnes gave herself up fully to her mission, and became the patron saint of the Czechs, the sick, the suffering and the poor, although too much time

Franz Kafka

passed before her devotion and goodness were properly appreciated. She was only made a saint in 1989. The Order of St. Clare occupied Agnes's monastery until the 15th century, when they were expelled by the Hussites. They returned only in 1626, but the Order was never able to live up to its celebrated past. Today, Agnes's monastery with the Church of St. Salvator has been converted into a gallery. In this splendid Gothic structure are displayed the master works of Czech Gothic artists. The neo-Renaissance **Rudolfinum**(65)** on Jan Palach Square, along with the National Theatre, is one of Prague's most celebrated concert venues. Its name is not linked to that great art-lover – Emperor Rudolf II, but to a different Rudolf, who was the Austrian crown prince. When the Rudolfinum was built between 1876-1884, and decorated with the work of Czech artists, it became the main centre of culture for Prague's German community, the German counterpart of the Czech National Theatre. The main concert hall in the Rudolfinum is the Dvořák Hall, which is considered to be one of the most important pieces of Czech architecture of the 19th century. Today, it is the main concert hall for the international *Prague Spring* music festival. Since 1901, the noble neighbour of the Rudolfinum has been the neo-Renaissance building of the **Art and Crafts Museum*(66)**. This contains one of the world's largest collections of glassware, but also worthy of note are the textile, furniture, porcelain, printed matter and photography collections.

Rabbi Löw and The Golem

The Golem

The most famous of Prague's Jews is undoubtedly Jehuda Löw ben Becalel (probably 1525-1609), also known as Rabbi Löw. This renowned Jewish philosopher, teacher and interpreter of the Talmud was the Rabbi of Prague during the reign of Emperor Rudolf II. It was Löw who is supposed to have created the Golem, a giant made from clay. When the clay was mixed with three other elements – water, air and fire, the Golem came to life, full of magical powers. According to the legend the Golem was awoken by a Shem (a plate with the true name of God), which was used in a way not unlike an electronic-chip card. This was inserted either into an opening above the Golem's eyes, or under his tongue. The clay giant is supposed to have lived in the rabbi's house and in the Old-New Synagogue and acted like a servant. The eventual fate of the Golem is shrouded in mystery. One version says that in an unexpected fit of anger he fell and smashed into pieces. Many people, however, are convinced that he is still hiding in the cellar of a house somewhere in Josefov, and is waiting for someone to find him again.

Wenceslas Square

THE NEW TOWN AND VYŠEHRAD

Despite its name, the 'New' Town is more than 650 years old. King Charles IV, who showed great generosity towards it, founded it in 1348 and granted it 350 hectares of land. At the time, the Old Town, Lesser Town and Hradčany put together weren't as large. Several centuries later, modern builders appreciated the timing of the wise ruler's decision. They didn't need to plan new streets and squares, as the ones built in Charles's time were wide and spacious enough to meet the demands of modern cities. Today, it is the New Town that gives Prague the genuine hallmark of a modern European metropolis. Vyšehrad is a completely different world. It is more the opposite of the New Town, a well-preserved picture of the illustrious history of the Czech nation.

Wenceslas Square as it was

Wenceslas Square today

The Entrance Hall of the National Museum

If a place is very busy, Czechs say that it's like 'Wenceslas', meaning that it's as bustling and noisy as Prague's **Wenceslas Square**. The shape and large dimensions of the square make it seem as if it is the result of a relatively new urban project. In fact, it emerged in the Middle Ages. Its founder Charles IV used it to join the fortifications of the Old and New Towns. The square's size was unheard of at the time. It is rectangular – 750 metres long and 60 metres wide. From the beginning the large space was filled with marketplaces. The upper end was where horses were traded, which led to the square being called the Horse Market. Later the main item bought and sold was grain. Today's name dates back to 1848, when the square was named after the Czech national saint and great patron St. Wenceslas. Large crowds gather beneath the huge **Statue of St. Wenceslas**(67)** riding on horseback, which adorns the upper end of the square, just as people congregate beneath the statue of Eros in London's Piccadilly Circus. The locals often agree to meet 'by the horse'. Slightly lower down than the statue is the **Memorial to the Victims of Communism*(68)**. Its location is no accident, as it was here in January 1969 that student Jan Palach set himself alight in protest against the occupation of Czechoslovakia by Warsaw Pact troops.

The dominant building on Wenceslas Square is the neo-Renaissance **National Museum**(69)** building, which since 1890 has stood at the highest point of the square. Before this date, the rich collections belonging to the National Museum (founded in 1818) were kept in various places all over Prague. The building is a worthy repository for the most valuable objects that the Czech nation has created over the course of many centuries. Its architectural style is full of symbolism relating to the richness of Czech history and culture. The imposing entrance hall is decorated with marble and granite. It has a huge double staircase and two-storey arcade, and is adorned with bronze statues of Princess Libuše, Přemysl the Ploughman, Prince Wenceslas and King Přemysl Otakar II. The hall known as the Pantheon is an impressive gallery of artistic works depicting the main figures and key events in Czech history. The museum also houses exhibitions focusing on prehistory, archaeology and old coins.

A look at the houses on Wenceslas Square makes it obvious that attempts have been made to present this, the most exposed space in Prague, in the best possible light. And for this reason we can find here various excellent examples of modern architecture. The outstanding Art Nouveau building on the square is the **Hotel Evropa*(70)**, halfway along the eastern side. The attractive facade of the neo-Romanesque **Wiehl House*(71)** built in 1896 on the corner

Hotel Evropa

Wenceslas Square

of Vodičkova Street was further enhanced by paintings created according to designs produced by Mikoláš Aleš. An innovative design was used for the **Lucerna Palace*(72)** on the corner of Štepánska Street. Lucerna Palace was the first building in Prague to be built with reinforced concrete. Its builder and owner was the grandfather of former-president Václav Havel. When he brought home the first drawings of the building's facade, his wife told him that it looked like a lantern ('lucerna', in Czech) and the name of the new building stuck. The Lucerna Palace is one of Prague's most famous concert venues – to the Czech capital it's something like the Olympia is to Paris. Many great names such as Louis Armstrong, Mireille Mathieu, Gilbert Bécaud, Tina Turner and Ray Charles have performed here.

The constructivist **Alfa Palace*(73)** built in 1928 on the western side of the square took its name from a popular café where people could dance. The Alfa Passage, from which until recently you could enter Prague's famous *Semafor* music hall, is an excellent escape route from the noise of Wenceslas Square to the Baroque **Franciscan Gardens*(74)**, a pleasant oasis of calm in the big city and one of the few preserved monastery gardens in Prague. The Franciscans used it to cultivate medicinal herbs. Today, the gardens have retained their original Baroque layout, in which there is still a fenced herb garden. From here you can see the **Church of the Virgin Mary of the Snow**(75)**. Although this is actually uncompleted, it is still monumental. It has the highest vaulting of all the Prague churches, at 34 metres. The church was begun in 1347 to commemorate the coronation of Charles IV, who

The Prague Passages

Prague is a city full of small passages, and this applies especially for Wenceslas Square and the streets attached to it. In the Old Town, the streets were linked by many passages back in the Middle Ages, and this architectural novelty was later carried over to the newer parts of the city. The first to emerge were in 1914, with the passages by the Hotel Ambassador and the Koruna Palace at the bottom end of Wenceslas Square. The most extensive maze of passages link the Rokoko Hotel and the Lucerna and Novák Palaces on the other side of the square. People go to the passages to shop, go to the cinema or theatre, or simply sit in a cosy café. They are an attractive space of human dimensions, unaffected by the weather, and with an idyllically comfortable and pleasant atmosphere. It's no wonder that new shopping centres are built in a similar style.

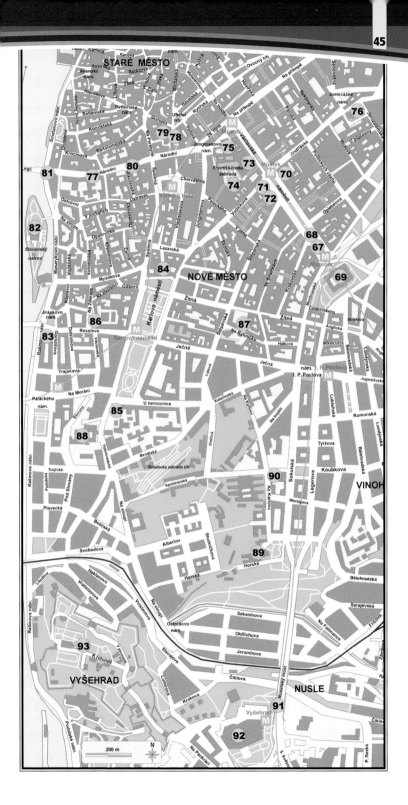

The Franciscan Gardens

said that it should become the coronation church. The main nave was completed in 1397, and was just the first part of a huge structure that was supposed to eclipse St. Vitus Cathedral in Prague Castle, and was planned to be 100 metres long. During the Hussite wars the building work was halted, however, before later being called off. The Church of the Virgin Mary of the Snow was the second-most important church for the Hussites after the Bethlehem Chapel. It was the scene of some fiery sermons from Jan Želivský. And it was following one of these in 1419 that a crowd set off for the New Town Hall, where the historic defenestration of the Catholic councillors took place. This spark ignited into the mass Hussite uprising. Inside the church is one of the tallest Baroque tiered altars in the Czech Republic, at 29-metres high. On the northern side, forming the entrance to the former monastery cemetery, is a Gothic gateway with the figure of the crowned Virgin Mary. The church was attached to the Franciscan monastery, to which the monks returned following the counter-Reformation.

Laterna magika

Senovážne Square, or the Haymarket, was built on the instructions of Charles IV, who chose the site for one of three marketplaces in the New Town. Nearby, in 1350, the Gothic **Church of St. Henry and Kunhuta*(76)** was built. This was one of the New Town's parish churches, and in 1817 was the scene of the wedding of composer Karl Maria von Weber to Karolína Brandtová, a soloist in the Estates Theatre opera. In 1476, a freestanding bell tower – St. Henry's Tower – was built next to the church. On its upper floors is an attractive restaurant, where you can have a good meal directly below the half-tonne St. Mary bell, cast in 1518. From the 10th floor there is a splendid view over Prague. In 2003, a set of 10 bronze bells was installed in the tower.

Národní třída (National Boulevard) is a wide boulevard linking the lower end of Wenceslas Square to the banks of the Vltava river and the Legion Bridge. It was built in 1781, and follows the course of the old castle moat. In 1870, it was named after Emperor Ferdinand V, who was the last monarch to have the Czech crown placed on his head. When he was removed from the throne in 1848, he continued to live in Prague Castle. During his unexpected retirement he often went for walks along his favourite street. Differing in age and style from the modern Národní třída is the Baroque **Church of St. Ursula*(77)** (1722) and above all the **Platýz Palace*(78),** where you can cut through to Uhelný trh, or Coal Market Square. Behind the Imperial-style facade hides a medieval palace, which was begun in 1347 for one of Charles IV's courtiers – Prince Frederick of Burgundy. The palace was bought in 1586 by Jan Platejs, the privy councillor of Emperor Rudolf II, and is named after him. Today, the palace is used for cultural and business purposes. Next to the palace is the noteworthy 12th century **Church of St. Martin in the Wall*(79).** It got its strange name because the church nave was incorporated into the town walls. In 1414, a priest called Jan of Hradec was the first to preside over the so-called 'communions in both kinds'. This means that the wor-

The National Theatre

shippers were not only offered the communion bread, but were also allowed to drink the wine from the altar in a chalice, which became the main symbol of the Hussites. The church now belongs to the Evangelical Church of the Czech Brethren. If you are on Národní třída, you shouldn't miss the vault of the Baroque **Kaňka House*(80)**. There are always candles burning near the memorial here, because this is the spot where on November 17, 1989 the police brutally attacked a group of peacefully protesting students. This attack led to demonstrations across the country, which caused the rapid collapse of the totalitarian communist regime.

The splendid building of the **National Theatre***(81)** built in the Italian-Renaissance style means the same to Prague as La Scala does to Milan, or the Bolshoi Theatre in Moscow. It was built twice (see text in italics below) according to a project drawn up by architect Josef Zítek, who had won a public competition. The artistic decoration of the National Theatre was a matter of pride for the greatest Czech artists of the day. The stage curtain produced by Vojtech Hynais, on which are depicted various leading artists and craftsmen coming to work on the theatre, is not only a great work due to its size. The motif celebrates the enormous efforts the Czech people put into building the theatre. In 1983, an extension was built on to the theatre building with a glass facade. In a corner of Lažanský Palace opposite the theatre is perhaps the most famous Prague café – the **Slávia***, a favourite meeting place for Prague intellectuals, artists and bohemians.

Local people like going to **Slavic Island*(82)** on the Vltava river, thanks to the opportunity for pleasant walks in superb surroundings and the good cultural facilities on offer at Žofín Palace.

The Emergence of the Czech National Theatre

For the Czech people, the building of the National Theatre was seen as a great test of national independence. The idea of building a Czech theatre took hold in 1845, when a group of Czech nationalists demanded that the authorities should build it. Five years later a countrywide collection was organised. Volunteers went round with collecting boxes to gather enough money for the theatre, and when the first of 26 foundation stones was laid on May 16, 1868, it was the largest national event of the 19th century. The first stone was brought from Radhošť, a peak in the Beskyd Mountains, while the other stones came from the most sacred places in Bohemia and Moravia. The Czech community in the U.S.A. donated one of them. The eagerly-awaited grand opening of the Czech National Theatre took place on June 11, 1881, with a performance of Smetana's opera 'Libuše'. The Czech people were not able to enjoy their new theatre long, however. On Friday, August 12, smoke began to pour out of the theatre roof, and soon the whole building was in flames. Despite the efforts of the fire brigade, it was too late. The bad news about the devastating fire brought a surprising response. A collection was organised on the very same day. In ten days half a million gold crowns had been raised, and on September 18, 1883, the new theatre was again able to put on a performance of 'Libuše'.

The Rašínovo Embankment

The Dancing House

Great works have been put on here since the 19th century. In 1878, Antonín Dvořák gave his first formal concert here and ten years later it hosted the premiere of Bedrich Smetana's *My Country*. Lizst and Tchaikovsky also performed concerts here. The Žofín also has a beautiful ballroom. In this area the Vltava river is lined by a row of elegant houses, many in the Art Nouveau style. There is one that is very different from the rest, however. Looking at the **Dancing House*(83)** on the Rasínovo Embankment, you are given the impressive that something is wrong either with your sight, or with the builder. Its extravagant shape differs from traditional ideas about architecture. From the square, the house is divided into a pair of towers, which appear to be dancing together. For this reason it is often called *Ginger and Fred* after the famous dancing partners Ginger Rogers and Fred Astaire. There's no need to worry, however, that this avantgarde house will collapse from dancing. You can calmly visit the restaurant on the top floor, from where you can get a great view.

Charles Square is like a much calmer version of Wenceslas Square. This may be due to its location and its spacious park with its lush greenery. It's also a rectangular shape (although it is larger), and has the same 'godfather'. Charles Square was also laid out in the 14th century. Charles IV named it the *Forum Magnum* (Great Marketplace). The main sight in the square is the 14th century **New Town Hall**(84),** which stands on the shorter, northern side. In 1419, it was the scene of the defenestration of the councillors, which led to the Hussite uprising. On the other side of the square is a Renaissance building reconstructed in the Baroque style known as **Faust's House*(85).** This house is supposed to be haunted, thanks to the strange people who lived here and their experiments. In 1590, it belonged to Edward Kelley, Rudolf II's court alchemist. Between 1740-1770, it was the home of another experimenter Ferdinand A. Mladota. Sometimes flames were seen inside his laboratory, which horrified people took as a sign of the Devil. In the romantically inclined 19th

The New Town Hall

century, a story went round that Doctor Faust had lived and signed away his soul there.

In Reslova Street, which runs into the centre of Charles Square, is the Baroque Church of **St. Cyril and St. Methodius*(86).** Apart from being a valuable religious monument, it's interesting because it was the hiding place of the assassins of Nazi Reich Protector of Bohemia and Moravia Reinhard Heydrich. The Czech agents were hidden by Matěj Gorazd, the bishop of the Orthodox Church. The Gestapo found them, however, and following a fierce battle they all committed suicide to avoid falling into enemy hands. The Germans executed the brave bishop. In the crypt of the church with its still visible bullet holes is the *National Memorial to the Victims of the Heydrich Terror.*

On Na Rybníčku Street to the east of Charles Square is the Romanesque **Rotunda of St. Longin*(87).** According to legend, Longin was a Roman soldier who took part in the crucifixion of Jesus Christ. He was so moved by what he saw

that he left the army, and spent the rest of his life as a hermit. When he was finally tracked down, he was executed for desertion. Charles IV brought his mortal remains from Italy to Prague. The small sacral monument from the 13th century belonged to a settlement owned by monks from the Břevnov Monastery. At the time this stood outside the Prague walls but, along with the Rotunda, Charles's New Town later annexed it.

Na Slovanech, or **Emmaus Monastery**(88)** church, provides an unusual sight, with its peculiar concrete tower, which, although built according to the Gothic style, is very modern. It appeared in 1969, as a replacement for the part of the church destroyed by bombing in February 1945. Charles IV founded the monastery in 1347. He invited Benedictine monks from southern Europe who used Old Slavonic rather than Latin as their liturgical language. The church was consecrated in 1372 in the presence of the king. During the ceremony a passage was read out from the gospels about the meeting between Christ and two of his disciples on the road to Emmaus, which is how the monastery got its name.

The enlightened Charles IV also founded the nearby **Augustinian Monastery*(89)** on Ke Karlovu Street. The monastery includes a church dedicated to the Virgin Mary and St. Charlemagne the Great, which has an unusual octagonal shape, supposedly on the pattern of the burial chapel of Charlemagne the Great in Aachen in Germany. The original Gothic church was later given a Baroque makeover. The most striking feature of the building are the three domes constructed in 1575. The central dome with a diameter of 24 metres and a height of 19 metres has a superb Renaissance-style star vault. The church is a place of pilgrimage, and according to legend gives those who pray here happy thoughts. It is said that here Bedřich Smetana thought of melodies used in the opera the *Bartered Bride.* The monastery now houses the *Czech Police Museum.* Also on Ke Karlovu Street you shouldn't miss the **Villa America*(90)** built in 1720. In this historical building, also

The Emmaus Monastery

Karlov

known as the Michna Summer House, is the *Antonín Dvořák Museum,* dedicated to the famous Czech composer.

Soon after getting off the metro at a nearby station, you will see two of Prague's main modern sights. The relatively deep Nusel valley is spanned by the modern **Nusel Bridge*(91),** which connects the districts of Karlov and Pankrác, and was built between 1965-1974. The bridge rises 40 metres above the Botič stream. A total of 17 houses had to be demolished to make way for it, while some were left standing, even though the bridge passes directly over their roofs. The upper part of the bridge is for cars, and is part of the so-called north-south highway. Inside the tube runs the C line of the metro and the **Congress Centre*(92)**

The Nusel Bridge

The Congress Centre

is on the Pankrác side of the bridge. This was opened in 1981, when it was called the Palace of Culture. Although this huge structure is not exactly the local people's favourite building, it has been of great benefit to the city, as it has brought a good deal of profit from so-called conference tourism. The Congress Centre has played host to some important international conferences includ-

ing one organised by the International Monetary Fund and the World Bank in 2000. Its main halls are able to seat 4,500 people, with another 30 smaller halls for 1,500 delegates.

If the old Czech story is to be believed, then **Vyšehrad***(93)** is even older than Prague Castle. The story goes that Prince Krok founded Vyšehrad fort. His daughter Libuše, who become

The Church of St. Peter and St. Paul

The St. Martin Rotunda

The Leopold Gate

ruler after his death, made her famous prophecy here about the founding of Prague. The written history of Vyšehrad begins at the turn of the 11th century, when Prague Castle was already in existence. Some time after 1067, Prince (later King) Vratislav II decided to move his official residence here. During this period three Romanesque-style religious buildings appeared. The Church of St. Peter and St. Paul was built between 13th-14th centuries. The later Baroque-style church was replaced after 1885 by today's purely neo-Gothic structure. The 11th-century St. Martin's Rotunda, has retained its impressive Romanesque form. The name Vyšehrad (meaning 'High Castle') describes the appearance of this venerable place very well. The territory enclosed by the fort is on high ground. The area on the rocks above the river with the remains of a guardhouse is called Libuše's Bathing Pool, because according to legend the princess bathed here with her lovers, before throwing them from the rocks into the Vltava. Today's Vyšehrad is mainly the result of building work carried out in the 17th century, which changed the whole site into a *military stronghold*. It was enclosed by defensive walls, which were often put to the test. These walls provide you with an excellent view of the city.

The Vyšehrad Slavín

Vyšehrad is not only a monument to the earlier history of the Czech nation, but also the final

rest-place for some of its greatest sons and daughters. In the 1870s the Vyšehrad National Cemetery emerged on the site of earlier cemetery dating back to the 13th century. The main feature of the site is the Slavín communal tomb built in 1893. The first to be buried there was writer Július Zeyer, who was followed by Jaroslav Vrchlický, Václav Myslbek, Alfons Mucha, Jan and Rafael Kubelík, and dozens of other great Czech figures. Other famous names can be found on around 600 individual tombstones, for example, the Čapek brothers, Božena Němcová, Jan Neruda, Bedřich Smetana, Antonín Dvořák, Zdeněk Fibich, Mikoláš Aleš, Jaroslav Heyrovský, Karel Hynek Mácha, Vítěslav Nezval and Max Švabinský. Many more famous people from the past are buried at the Olšanský Cemetery in Žižkov. These include Czechs Jan Werich, Josef Lada, and Josef Mánes, along with some famous Slovaks such as Ján Kollár and Pavol Jozef Šafárik. In the eastern part of the Olšanský Cemetery is the Jewish Cemetery, where Franz Kafka is buried.

Graves on Slavín

THE PRAGUE SUBURBS

If you head out of the centre in any direction, you're sure to find something interesting. To the west is the ancient Břevnov Monastery, while a little further on is a former royal hunting ground and the Star Summer House. To the north of the centre on a bend on the Vltava river is the Holešovice Výstavisko (Exhibition Ground) and Stromovka Park, much loved by the locals. In Trója on the right bank of the Vltava are the prettily arranged Baroque castle, zoo and botanical gardens. On the southern edge of Prague is the former Zbraslav Monastery, which has been converted into a castle. And what shouldn't you miss in the eastern suburbs? Well, you should definitely check out the view from the Žižkov Television Mast and visit the National Monument on Vítkov.

Sightseeing Boat on the Vltava river

Holešovice and Letná

A bend in the Vltava river curves around the district of **Holešovice**. This primarily industrial part of Prague emerged in 1891 as the site of the Prague Jubilee Exhibition. After this successful event, the exhibition ground was extended with sights to attract tourists, forming the area now officially known as **Výstaviště (Exhibition Ground)**(94).** The dominant building in this area is the Industrial Palace, which covers an area of 300,000 square metres. The biggest tourist attraction, however, is Křižík's Fountain, which delights those who come to see it with its synchronised music and light show. It was built for the people of Prague by the Czech 'Edison' František Křižík, and was part of the afore-mentioned exhibition. Its repertoire of impressive 'fountain concerts' includes, for example, Dvořák's opera *The Water Nymph,* along with *Swan Lake* and *Carmen.* In the Lapidarium National Museum by the Exhibition Ground's main entrance, you can see a representative collection of the best works

produced by Czech sculptors for over nine centuries. You should also see Marold's Panorama, the largest work of its kind in the Czech Republic, which depicts the Battle of Lipany in 1434. This huge painting, produced in 1898 by Luděk Marold, covers an area of more than a thousand square metres. Given the various pieces of military equipment around, you feel as if you were standing in the midst of the battle fought between Hussite and Catholic Crusader forces. Next to the Exhibition Ground is the spacious **Stromovka Park*(95).** One of Prague's largest green areas, it emerged as a result of the conversion of the former Royal Hunting Ground into an English-style park. On the south-west edge of the park is the Governor's Summer House with its romantic neo-Gothic look.

It's only a stone's throw from the Exhibition Ground to the **Trade Fair Palace**(96),** which was built in 1928 as the first functionalist structure in Prague, and was the second largest such

The Trade Fair Palace

Vltava Embankment

H. Rousseau: Self Portrait

Sparta Prague Shop in Letná

building in the world at that time. It attracted a great deal of attention from architects, and Le Corbusier, for example, was among its admirers. To mark the opening of the palace, Alfons Mucha's *Slav Epic* was put on show here. Today, this grandiose work by the Art Nouveau painter is on show at Moravský Krumlov Castle in Moravia. The Trade Fair Palace was built for exactly the purpose its name suggests, but when Brno replaced Prague as the main centre for such events the palace had to find a new role. In 1974, the building was badly burned, and it was threatened with demolition. Fortunately, a better solution was found, and after the expensive reconstruction work was completed in 1995, it was decided that the building should house collections of modern art from the *National Gallery*. This gives you an excellent opportunity to see works by great artists, including Picasso, Rousseau, Klimt, Munch, Zrzavý and Cézanne. There is also an extensive collection of impressionist paintings.

The **Letná Gardens*(97)** are in an excellent location - right next to Hradčany. It's an ideal place to unwind after the demanding tourist marathon around the sights of Prague Castle. A spacious park with many long pathways takes up most of the gardens, which cover an area of 25 hectares. On the southern side, the gardens end where the ground falls away steeply, and from here a famous view of the Old Town and the Vltava river opens out. Here you quickly grasp why Prague is called the city of a hundred spires. From the area near the Metronome, with its large pendulum rod, you can admire the distinct line of Josefov, from the Čechov Bridge to

View of Letná from the Hanavský Pavilion

the Old Town Square. Until 1962, a large stone statue of 'Uncle Joe' Stalin kept watch over Prague from this spot. To get the best view of the Vltava bridges, however, you need to go to the terrace in front of the Hanavský Pavilion in the southwest corner of Letná (summer) Gardens. In the same gardens is the starkly modern building of the **National Technical Museum**(98),** built in 1908. Its extensive collection is among the largest of its kind in Europe. Of special value is the exhibition displaying many old forms of transportation. Here you can find, for example, the railway carriage of Emperor Franz Joseph, and the Blériot aeroplane in which Jan Kašpar made an historic early flight within the territory of today's Czech Republic, from Pardubice to Prague.

Břevnov and White Mountain

The Benedictine **Břevnov Monastery**(99)** amazes us with its splendid Baroque style. Inside the building is hidden the oldest Czech monastery, which was founded in 993 by Boleslav II together with St. Vojtěch. In the 11th century, the monks built a stone abbey church, of which only the Romanesque crypt survives, beneath the Church of St. Margaret. This Baroque church from the first half of the 18th century is the greatest work of the Dienzenhofer father-and-son team, whose input can also clearly be seen in the monastery building. Part of this structure is the famous Theresian Hall, which commemorates a private visit made by Empress Maria Theresia and her husband Francis Stephen of Lorraine in 1753.

West of Břevnov is the flat-topped hill known as the **White Mountain*(100),** which holds unpleasant memories for the Czechs. A stone cairn commemorates the important battle that took place

here on November 8, 1620. This was won by troops fighting on behalf of the Catholic Hapsburgs, who defeated an army of Czech Protestants. The outcome of this memorable clash on the White Mountain determined the history of the Czech people for three long centuries. After their victory, the jubilant Catholics chose a nearby site to built a chapel, which in 1714 was extended into the elegant **Church of the Virgin Mary Victorious*(101)** by master of the Baroque style Jan (also Giovanni) Santini. North of the White Mountain, you will find the walls of a former hunting ground. Inside is a noteworthy 16th-century Renaissance building, whose plan is shaped like a five-pointed star, and is therefore called the **Star Summer House**(102).** This was

The Star Summer House

built for Archduke Ferdinand of Austria. Rumour has it that it was for a secret wife of humble birth, but it is easier to believe that it was meant for lively parties following a successful day's hunting. It is said that the hunting ground did not just contain animals typical for this part of the world, but was also home to a dozen lions. The summerhouse now contains a small museum dedicated to the novelist Alois Jirásek and painter Mikoláš Aleš.

Břevnov Monastery

Smíchov

Smíchov

Zbraslav

Zbraslav Castle

Mozart and Prague

Prague can be proud of the fact that it several times welcomed the greatest musical genius of the 18th century – Wolfgang Amadeus Mozart (1756-91). Mozart came to Prague for the first time in 1787, in order to personally conduct his opera The Marriage of Figaro, which was a great success at the Estates (then Nostic) Theatre. He signed a contract for a spring season of a new opera with theatre impresario Pasqual Boldini, and so Mozart's famous Don Giovanni came into being. The new opera had its world premiere on October 29, 1787, again at the Estates Theatre, with the great Mozart again wielding the conductor's baton. However, Mozart's final visit to Prague wasn't such a great success. On September 6, 1791, the clearly ailing composer put on a celebratory performance of his opera La Clemenza di Tito for the coronation of Leopold II as Czech king. The appropriate recognition from the emperor's court wasn't forthcoming, however. Nine days after Mozart's death on December 5, 1791, Prague staged a huge memorial concert at the Church of St. Nicholas in the Lesser Town. Four thousand people came to pay their respects.

The Monastery Church of St. James

The predominantly industrial district of **Smíchov** on the left bank of the Vltava river has completely merged into the historical centre of the city. It is famous mainly for the largest brewery in Prague, which produces the popular *Staropramen* beer. The 17th century **Bertramka Villa**(103)**, a cosy building with its country-house appearance, is home to a museum dedicated to one of Wolfgang Amadeus Mozart's visits to Prague. František Xaver Dušek and his wife Jozefína bought the villa in 1784. Both made a living from music – Jozefina was a singer and František played the piano and taught music. For this reason, they turned their homely summer residence in Smíchov into a celebrated music salon. In 1787, the Dušeks played host to their family friend Mozart, and it was that the famous composer finished off his opera *Don Giovanni*.

Zbraslav Castle**(104) is located on the left bank of the Vltava river, on the southern edge of Prague. This residence of the bishop of Prague was acquired in 1268 by King Přemysl Otakar II. His heir Wenceslas II had different plans for this hunting residence, however. He decided that it would become the Cistercian monastery *Aula Regia*, and, at the same time, the final resting place of Bohemia's rulers. In 1305, Wenceslas was laid to rest in the crypt of the Church of St. Mary, and was followed by the next 13 rulers of the Premyslid and Luxembourg royal houses. The monastery's development was halted by the Hussites, who set fire to it in 1420. The Zbraslav Cistercians experienced yet more suffering during the Thirty Years War. In the 18th century, a new chapter in the monastery's history was begun, when it was given a Baroque makeover. The better times didn't last long, however, and in 1787 the abandoned monastery was converted into a sugar mill. In 1825, reconstruction work was begun on the derelict castle building. This demanding task was carried out in several stages, to give the castle the splendid appearance it has today. The eminent Slovak architect Dušan Jurkovič had a hand in the restoration work carried out between 1912-26. Today, the castle, houses a rich collection of Asian art that belongs to the National Gallery. You can also visit the monastery's Church of St. James the Elder. Despite its Baroque reconstruction work, several original early-Gothic features have been preserved. Since 1925, the church has housed a monument to Přemysl the Ploughman, inside which is a box containing the skulls of Wenceslas II, Wenceslas III, and Eliška Přemyslovna.

Troja

Inside there are four thousand square metres of walls and ceilings covered with valuable paintings by Italian masters. Apart from this, there are collections belonging to the Prague Gallery, focusing on old-style printing and maps of the Far East. The castle also has a carefully cultivated French Garden. The entire castle territory can be nicely viewed from above. All you have to do is visit the Troja **Botanical Garden**(106).** The view can be had from the Baroque chapel standing on the historical St. Clare Vineyard, dating back to the 17th century. The Botanical Garden itself emerged much later than the vineyard. Work began here in 1968, but the garden was only opened to the public in 1992. The biggest draw is the Fata Morgana (Mirage) Tropical Greenhouse, which allows you to see what an African virgin rainforest or semi-desert looks like. In the refrigerated part of the complex you can experience the conditions found in the Andes Mountains.

The enigma that is Troja Castle

The name of the Prague district of Troja, on the right bank of the Vltava river, was arrived at by accident, due to a mistake connected with **Troja Castle**(105).** The Baroque statues on the castle's monumental outer staircase were mistakenly thought to represent the heroes of the famous Trojan wars. They were actually meant to portray a different ancient mythological theme – the battle between the gods of Mt. Olympus and the Titans. Troja Castle was built at the end of the 17th century for Count Šternberk, in the style of an Italian Baroque villa. The castle is a piece of art in itself, but it is also overflowing with great works.

Troja Castle

Gaston the Wanderer

The flood that hit Prague Zoo in the summer of 2002 enabled a group of seals to escape. Three females were recaptured relatively quickly, but a male called Gaston continued on his quest for freedom, swimming three hundred kilometres along the swollen Vltava river. When they finally captured him in the German town of Lutterstadt, Gaston was completely exhausted, and on the return journey to Prague he died. Gaston's escape produced a big reaction. A children's book was written about him in Germany that was later adapted for the stage in a play called 'Swim, Gaston, Swim!' The play had a very successful run at the Saxon State Opera House in Dresden. Three years after his death, Gaston returned to Troja. A bronze statue of him sticks its curious head above the waters of a small lake located inside the restored zoo.

Vinohrady and Žižkov

The district of **Vinohrady** emerged on the site of some former vineyards, which were planted by Charles IV in the 14th century. Such old vineyards are now mainly a thing of the past, although there is a small area remaining near **Gröbe's Villa*(108)** in Havlíčkový sady, with the restoration of the St. Clare Vineyard. A major building project on the royal vineyards began in the first half of the 19th century. In 1849, there was a separate village here called *Královské Vinohrady (Royal Vineyards)*, which became a town in 1879. Although Vinohrady didn't become a part of Prague until 1922, with its 90,000 inhabitants it was smaller than only two of the Prague towns. The constructionist **Czech Radio*(109)** building (1932) stands at the lower

The St. Clare Vineyard in Troja

The Church of the Most Sacred Heart

The Vineyard above Troja Castle

In front of the Czech Radio Building

Prague Zoo**(107) in Troja covers an area of 60 hectares next to the castle. It isn't one of the Czech Republic's oldest zoos, as it was only opened in 1931, but it is definitely one of the most attractive. It is home to around four thousand animals belonging to approximately five hundred species and has enjoyed great success in breeding various rare and endangered species. In 2004, as many as 415 young mammals, birds and reptiles were born here, and the zoo is famous especially for its outstanding success in breeding the Przewalski horse, a wild breed that would otherwise have become extinct.

end of Vinohradská Street. During the Prague uprising in May 1945, it was the scene of the heaviest street fighting with the German forces. Another battle for the building took place during the invasion by Warsaw Pact forces in August 1968. Of architectural interest is the monumental **Church of the Most Sacred Heart of Our Lord*(110)** on Jiří z Poděbrad (George of Poděbrady) Square. This looks like a huge sailing ship, and is considered to be one of the most important religious Czech buildings of the 20th century. It was consecrated in 1932 by the archbishop of Prague himself.

Žižkov Television Mast

Žižkov

The National Monument on Vítkov

This peculiar-looking monument was built between 1928 and the beginning of WWII. It was supposed to symbolise the glory - and become the final resting place - of members of the Czechoslovak legions, who fought for the allies in the First World War, and also later came into conflict with Soviet troops. The Communists adopted it, nonetheless. In 1949, the body of an unknown Soviet soldier from the Dukla battlefield in the Carpathian mountains was buried here, while in 1954, it became the site of the mausoleum of Klement Gottwald, Czechoslovakia's first Communist president. Originally, the plan was to build a Lenin-style mausoleum on Letenská plan, which would also be used for military reviews and May Day celebrations. Just like Lenin, Gottwald was embalmed after his death, before being placed inside the monument. There always had to be plenty of light in the place where his body was on show, to make him look alive. He was kept 'in condition' by a permanent team of 70-120 doctors and make-up artists. Soviet specialist Professor Mardashev, who also embalmed Bulgarian Communist leader Georgi Dimitrov, led the team until 1955. By 1962, Gottwald's personality cult had weakened. The

mausoleum was closed, and Gottwald's body was cremated.

Jan Žižka

Žižkov Television Tower*(113) at 216 metres high is Prague's tallest structure. It was built between 1985-92. There is a viewing gallery at 97 metres, while at 63 metres you'll find a restaurant.

The district of **Žižkov*(111)** emerged in the 19th century as a poor area. Today's Žižkov has two main sights – the National Monument and the Television Tower, which can both by seen from many parts of the entire city. The bronze statue of Jan Žižka in front of the **National Monument on Vítkov*(112)** is impossible to miss, as it's the largest such statue in the world. It is nine metres high and weighs in at 16 and a half tonnes. Žižka's statue is in the right place, because it was here on Vítkov hill that the legendary Hussite commander led his troops to their first great victory over the Catholic Crusaders on July 14, 1420. The entire district is now named after him. The

The National Monument on Vítkov

A tram café

Travelling to and from Prague

Prague can be reached from the rest of the world by all the usual means of transport apart from by sea. It's central position in both the Czech Republic and Europe makes it an important transport hub, bisected by many main European routes. Its single international airport 'Ruzyně' is located on the western edge of the city, 12 km from the centre. This is one of the busiest airports in Central Europe, with 10 million passengers using its services every year, and direct routes to more than 100 other airports all over the world. There are also nine rail routes leading into the city, including international ones linking Western and Eastern Europe, while the city centre is home to four large railway stations. Hlavné nádraží (Main railway station) and Prague-Holešovice station deal with both international and domestic routes. Other domestic journeys begin or end at the Masaryk and Prague-Smíchov stations. International and domestic buses use Prague-Florenc bus station, while the bus station next to the Smíchov railway station also handles domestic routes. There are four main road routes leading to Prague, although only the D1 highway to Brno reaches an international border (with Slovakia). This road is extremely busy, however, and

A train leaving Masaryk Railway Station

the scene of an unfortunate number of accidents. Prague still lacks a main ring road. Although the Vltava river flows through Prague, it doesn't have water links comparable to those of Vienna and Bratislava on the Danube. You can, however, take sightseeing boat trips on Prague's picturesque river, or, at certain times of year, sail to places near Prague, such as Slapy or Mělník.

City Transport

Driving into the centre of Prague isn't a good idea. You'll have to deal with the same problems as in any other large city, and the densely built-up historical city centre makes things even trickier. There aren't enough parking places in the centre, and the system of one-way streets and busy main roads is a real headache. The best thing to do is to park your car outside the city centre somewhere near a metro station, from where you can quickly and comfortably get to all the most important tourist locations. The Prague metro has been in service since 1974, and has three different-coloured lines with 47 stations and 54 km of track. The metro is co-ordinated with a comprehensive public transport system above ground, consisting of 199 bus routes and 35 tramlines, which can take you to every corner of the city. It makes sense to buy an all-day or multi-day ticket, which you can use on all forms of public transport. Of course, you can also take taxis, but if you do, make sure that you agree on the fare before you set off, or you could be fleeced. The best way to see the historical centre of Prague, however, is on foot, as there are several kilometres of pedestrian routes. You can use one of these to get from Wenceslas Square to Prague Castle, for example.

Recreational Routes

When visiting Prague, you can mix things up a little with a pleasant trip on the Vltava river. Guided boat trips leave from the quay near the Čechov Bridge. In summer, the river port on the Rašín Embankment offers old-fashioned steamboat trips to Trója, Mělník and Slapy. A really romantic option is to climb on board the Posázavský Pacifik miniature train, which will take you to a charming world of hiking opportunities in the Sázava river valley. The train leaves from the Main railway station (Hlavné nádražie) and terminates at Čerčany.

Accommodation

Despite the wide range of hotels and guesthouses of all categories, finding accommodation in Prague is a big problem. This is because the Czech capital is one of the most popular tourist destinations in Europe, with more than 3 million visitors from abroad every year. It's best to book your accommodation in advance to avoid major hassles. You can book a room via the Internet or through one of the official tourist information offices. Staying in the historical centre of Prague is indeed romantic, but it comes at a price. If you want cheaper accommodation, it's better to try hotels and guesthouses located a good way out, and if you can find one near a metro station, you'll still be able to get to the centre in just a few minutes. In summer, the number of rooms increases when university halls of residence are freed up. One very pleasant option is to stay on one of the boat hotels anchored to the banks of the Vltava river.

Food and Drink

Prague has a large number of restaurants, pubs and cafés. You can find Italian, Chinese, Indian and French restaurants, but it would be a big mistake to come here and not try real Czech cuisine. Czech food is excellent, and very tasty, although you should be warned that it doesn't

Prague Pubs — The U Fleků Pub

The popular U Pinkasů pub (Pinkas Cellar) on Jungmanovo Square has been serving the famous Pilsner Urquell beer since 1843. It also deserves a mention because it was a favourite haunt of the Good Soldier Švejk, the main character from Jaroslav Hašek's novel of the same name. The real mecca for 'Švejkists', however, is the U Kalicha (The Chalice) restaurant in the southern part of the New Town (12, Na Bojišti Street), whose landlord was, according to Hašek's famous novel, Pálivec from Pilsen. Another famous Prague pub is U Fleků (11, Křemencova Street, - just south of Národni třída), which serves the celebrated Flekovský dark beer, brewed on the premises in Prague's smallest brewery since 1499. The beer got its current name in 1762, when Jakub Flekovský bought the brewery. The largest beer hall is a venue for traditional Prague cabaret shows.

always conform to what you might expect. Czech dishes are very similar to those of the country's central-European neighbours. Very popular here are soups, especially those consisting of a meaty broth with noodles. If you ask the locals about Czech national dishes, many will tell you about the popular combination of roast pork *(bravčoví pečený maso)*, sauerkraut *(kyselé zelí)* and 'knedlík', which is a kind of light dumpling made from either bread *(houskový knedlík)* or potatoes *(bramborový knedlík)*. Knedlík also goes well with smoked meat *(údený maso)*, roast duck *(pečena kačka)*, or the also extremely popular sirloin of beef in cream *(svíčková na smotaně)*, which consists of slices of stewed beef in a mild cream sauce with cranberries. Most traditional Czech dishes are unthinkable without a glass of beer. It can be said that the 'golden nectar' is the Czech national drink. Indeed, Czechs are the biggest beer-drinkers in the world. Beer also goes well with the so-called 'beer cheese' *(pivný sýr)*, or spicy sausage in vinegar *(špekáček v octu)*, which everybody calls a 'drowned man' *(utopenec)*. A word about prices ... In the centre of Prague the prices are for tourists, and therefore quite high. Further out, the prices fall considerably, but not the quality. If you want to eat like the locals, you should try a bratwurst-style sausage *(klobáska)* or frankfurter from one of the traditional stalls on Wenceslas Square.

Old Town Gallery

two camps: Sparta and Slavia. Sparta's ground is the Letná Stadium, while Slavia play their home games in Vršovice. You should also definitely go to see an ice hockey match. After all, a country that has been world champions several times really ought to play excellent ice hockey.

Culture and Entertainment

There are so many cultural and entertainment options in Prague that there is something for everyone. Prague theatre shows are traditionally excellent, although the classical drama form is mainly for Czechs. Foreign visitors tend to go for the opera, ballet, and non-traditional stage forms such as the so-called black theatre, plus pantomime and multimedia 'magic lantern' shows. In the past, cabaret was very popular, but today, musicals are all the rage. The main venue for classical music concerts is the Rudolfinum, while concerts staged at the city's churches have a special charm. Prague's older citizens prefer to listen to performances of Dvořák's or Smetana's works performed by brass bands, which are particularly good in the Czech Republic. One of the best-known songs in the world *Škoda lásky (A Waste of Love)* is also Czech. Young people, of course, prefer other types of music. Following the Velvet Revolution in 1989, world-famous rock and pop stars swarmed in. The most famous concert venue is the Lucerna. It is said that any Czech musician who can sell out the Lucerna has really made it big.

Prague is also a good place for sports fans. When it comes to football, the city is divided into

Musical Prague

Prague's premier event in terms of classical music is the Prague Spring International Music Festival, which is made up of a series of concerts running from May to June. At the beginning of the summer, Prague belongs to Mozart, with several concerts celebrating his outstanding music. In October, Prague plays host to jazz fans, who are spoilt for choice at the International Jazz Festival.

Souvenirs from Prague

Prague's souvenir shops have all sorts of things to choose from. Let's begin by telling you what you shouldn't buy. Russian matrioshka nesting dolls and Soviet officers' caps are definitely not the real Prague. Quality Bohemian crystal, porcelain, and jewellery made from Czech garnets, however, are quintessential Prague gifts. If you pack some beer (preferably Prague's Staropramen) or a bottle of the typical herbal liqueur Becherovka, you'll certainly bring home a genuine piece of beautiful Prague.

Index